The Leadership
road less travelled

Leading as God intended you to

ANDY PECK

CWR

'Leadership is never straightforward. Any leader will tell you that she or he has had to navigate many unexpected twists and turns in the road. No matter where you are on the leadership journey, there is always more to learn, and there is always something unexpected ahead. Andy Peck's new book draws on his own experience of these twists and turns, but also mines the experience of many other leaders whom He has interviewed and listened to on the subject. This book is a trustworthy sat-nav for those of us who need as much help and wisdom as we can get, to be the leaders that God is calling us to be.'

Malcolm Duncan, Senior Pastor of Gold Hill Baptist Church, Theologian-in-Residence for Essential Christian and Spring Harvest.

Published 2018 by CWR, Waverley Abbey House, Waverley Lane, Farnham, Surrey GU9 8EP, UK. CWR is a Registered Charity – Number 294387 and a Limited Company registered in England – Registration Number 1990308.
The rights of Andy Peck to be identified as the author of this work has been asserted by him in accordance with the Copyright, Designs and Patents Act 1988.
For a list of National Distributors, visit www.cwr.org.uk/distributors
Scripture references are taken from the Holy Bible, New International Version® Anglicised, NIV® Copyright ©1979, 1984, 2011 by Biblica, Inc.® Used by permission. All rights reserved worldwide.
Scripture taken from The Message: Copyright © 1993, 1994, 1995, 1996, 2000, 2001, 2002. Used by permission of NavPress Publishing Group.
Concept development, editing, design and production by CWR.
Every effort has been made to ensure that this book contains the correct permissions and references, but if anything has been inadvertently overlooked the Publisher will be pleased to make the necessary arrangements at the first opportunity. Please contact the Publisher directly.
Cover image: Melanie Ray
Printed in the UK by Linney
ISBN: 978-1-78259-801-5

The Leadership Road Less Travelled

Acknowledgements

My thanks to the 600 plus leaders who have been my guests on *The Leadership File* over the last 12 years. All the ideas in this book are my own, but many have been formed through listening to men and women wiser and more experienced than me. Thanks for blessing my listeners on Premier Christian Radio with your time and insight.

My thanks too to CWR, my employers who supported the radio work for 11 of those years, giving me the time and covering my travel to serve in this way and with whom I have led courses on leadership. I hope the courses I have delivered have been enhanced because of the radio experience.

Thanks to Rebecca Berry at CWR, whose editing has made this a much stronger and more readable book. Particular thanks to Lynette Brooks, Publishing Director at CWR, and John Buckeridge, Deputy Chief Executive at Premier, for making this book possible.

Contents

Introduction

The subject of leadership actually leaves me quite cold.

These might sound like strange words from someone who has hosted a leadership show on Premier Christian Radio[1] for 12 years, comprising over 300 hours of interviews… words stranger still given that they begin a book on this very topic!

However, it's not leadership as an academic discipline that interests me, but leading – the influencing of others to bring about change. It's the *stories* of leading that excite me. I think of the guests that have appeared on my radio show: one of my first ever guests, Kurt Erickson, church planting among the homeless in London; Archie Coates, resurrecting a dying church in Brighton to a state of vibrancy; Ruth Dearnley, rescuing sex-trafficked women and restoring their lives; Graham Tomlin, pioneering styles of theological education (which is now one of the most popular among Anglican ordinands); Rick Warren, planting a church in Orange County with three people, which is now around 25,000; Louise Donkin, leading a student movement that has changed government legislation towards a fairer and more just approach; John Sutherland, one-time Borough Police Commander of Southwark leading thousands of police officers; Helen Shannon, pioneering work among the poor in urban London; Anita Deyneka, leading her late husband's ministry to serve emerging leaders in the former Soviet Union…

The list goes on, and I'm constantly amazed.

But as aware as I am of these great stories, I feel for those who feel it's not going quite so well – people who started on the right road, but later ground to a halt. Those who found the people they tried to lead to be unresponsive or hostile. People searching for answers because they know how vital leadership is, but can't find the way. I think of

Christians in businesses and public life who face the challenge of living for Jesus where He has placed them, but wonder if they might be better off keeping their faith quiet, lest they incur the wrath of those they work with or serve. I think of church leaders who feel like they are wading through proverbial treacle. The charity I serve, CWR, conducted a survey of church pastors with the Evangelical Alliance in 2000, and found that 50% of respondents had considered quitting in the previous two years. Chances are it's crossed the mind of someone you know who leads a church. Maybe even yours?

Leading others can be tough. I say these things with some feeling. *The Leadership File* radio show wasn't just born out of an awareness that shedding light on leadership might be helpful. Some years into the show, I realised I was slowly able to make sense of a seven-year stint in church pastoral leadership that had left me perplexed and confused. I had since moved on to other leadership, but this had been a big puzzle.

I feel I should explain. Many of the ingredients for a long lasting pastoral ministry were in place. I had served for four years in itinerant student ministry with UCCF, leading to three years as Assistant Minister at a 500-member independent Baptist church in Bournemouth, a church with a strong reputation for biblical ministry. God had even provided that I work with a senior pastor, who was a good friend and fellow Everton fan: the irrepressible Steve Brady. I had met my wife, Nic, while in student work on a summer team in that very town, and so married life had begun within this environment. What a blessing.

From there I moved to what seemed a dream ministry job, working for Waterfront Church, Southampton, which had been planted imitating the inspirational Willow Creek Community Church in Chicago (a church I had visited in 1991, which had by then formed an association in the UK). Willow Creek had blossomed using a strategy of arranging its activities around reaching people who were not believers, with its Sundays devoted to what became known as 'seeker services'. Waterfront had been going for three years when I joined as Associate Minister on a one-year contract, with the hope that their approach to reach the unchurched in Southampton would flourish to the point where I could sign up for longer.

But the year was not smooth. I arrived in July and out of the blue, the founding pastor announced that he would be leaving that November to move into counselling. I admired him and had looked forward to working on this project. The church was 'ticking over' with around 50 in attendance, but the initial drive to see friends come to faith had largely gone, and the seeker-targeted model (whereby the main morning service had no sung worship) didn't seem to be working.

The lay church leaders were clearly exhausted, with a number resigning during the year. It made little financial sense to remain in the church office we were renting, so we moved to the garage/study of a church member. It was clear that the concern for 'the lost' was all-encompassing, and there was little appetite for regular worship. As a young pastor, I didn't have the bottle to challenge the church culture.

And then I believe God spoke. I was in the church office one afternoon, preparing for a talk, and words I hadn't planned came to mind in a way that I have come to recognise as God. The words were: 'time to move on'.

What? This was my dream job! I couldn't imagine anything else matching my ministry desires at that stage of my life. This was a rare and special opportunity to follow a dream that had been gestating for at least four years. And yet the more I considered it, the wiser this seemed. I hated leaving the church at such a time, but had been meeting with a friend, John Balchin, who had been a lecturer when I was at Bible College. He reminded me: 'If God is moving you on, He will take care of His Church!' Little did I know that this would be my last full-time pastoral position.

I had been in touch with a Surrey-based Baptist minister, Paul Adams, who had led a leadership evening at Waterfront Church. Hearing of my impending resignation, he invited me to work at his church part-time while I awaited my next posting. Thankfully, my wife secured a teaching job, and in time I was able to preach and serve in a part-time capacity at Banstead Baptist Church while I looked at a number of church situations seeking pastors: two in West Sussex, one in Hull, a church plant in Northamptonshire, one in north Hertfordshire and two in the Bristol area. On some occasions it was 'meet the leadership'; on others it was 'preach with a view' (a system common in independent churches). But there was always something that didn't feel right, and each time I pulled out of the process, eventually realising that it wasn't that I hadn't found the right church, but I wasn't the right person.

I had been on the road to pastoral ministry from summer 1984 (when I'd headed for Bible College, assuming pastoral ministry was a likely route). I loved preaching, teaching, discipleship and evangelism, but somehow hadn't found a niche. Here I was, 15 years later, concluding that I needed to look elsewhere. Alongside my interviews with Christians in leadership were nagging personal questions to do with calling, the style of leadership required in a local church, and what God was looking for from me and from others who serve Him.

My journey can be summed up with reference to a TV advert screened in 1986 to publicise the merits of *The Guardian* newspaper. The viewer observes a menacing looking youth dressed in jeans, a bomber jacket and Doc Martens running along the street. A second camera angle shows him running towards a businessman carrying a brief case, who turns and grips his case to his chest, alarmed at what appears to be an attempted mugging. The final scene is shot from an elevated camera, which reveals that a crane is about to drop a load of bricks onto the businessman. What seemed to be a mugging was actually the youth saving his life. The narrator finishes with the line: 'It's only when you get the full picture you can fully understand what is going on.'

I found that the Bible gives a full picture when it comes to how God wants us to understand the subject of leadership. But like that advert for *The Guardian*, many believe something entirely different is going on. They assume leadership is one thing because they see leadership through the lens of their own experience, and their own ideas and beliefs about who God is.

I invite you to explore with me what I am calling 'the leadership road less travelled', an approach to leadership modelled by Jesus, and contrast it with the way we are perhaps tempted to walk. I hope you will discover how to walk this road, and how it will impact how you view yourself. You will learn how to be energised for the journey, how to journey with others, find focus, develop a healthy mindset, withstand adversity and arrive at your destination.

Everyone's experience of leading is unique, and of course my journey is not yours. But I hope that some things I have picked up may save you from similar mistakes, and inspire you to great things with God. Your area of leadership may seem relatively small; perhaps it's a family, or a small group, a sports team or a department of a business. It may be larger; a local church, a charity, a business, even a country? Or maybe you're new to the idea, and exploring what leading might mean for you. Your leading may have its own method of measuring 'success', or it may not. But leading in the way of Jesus will allow you to have success in His eyes, the only metric that truly matters.

My book's title is inspired by the title of the bestselling book *The Road Less Travelled* by the late M. Scott Peck[2] (no relation), which helped so many handle life's challenges. That title was inspired by Robert Frost's poem, *The Road Not Taken*, in particular its final lines:

> *'Two roads diverged in a wood, and I—*
> *I took the one less traveled by,*
> *And that has made all the difference.'*

May this be true for you.

My road so far

The book includes a lot of autobiography, but not in order. If you're the kind of reader that wants to know what goes where, the order is as follows:

1981–1984 Wye College, London University BSc (Hons) Agricultural Economics

1984–1986 University of Cambridge Diploma in Religious Studies, taken at London Bible College

1987–1988 Executive Officer at Intervention Board for Agricultural Produce

1988–1992 UCCF staff worker, training leaders of CUs in the south of England

1992–1995 Assistant Minister at Lansdowne Baptist Church, a church of 550 members in Bournemouth, with responsibility for outreach

1995–1996 Associate Pastor of Waterfront Church, a 50-member church plant looking to reach the unchurched in Southampton

1996–1999 Part-time Bible trainer at Banstead Baptist Church (350 members), now Christchurch, Banstead, Surrey

1999–2006 Deputy Editor at *Christianity* magazine, based at Premier Christian Radio, London

2006–present Teaching team of CWR, and (from 2005) Host, *The Leadership File*, Premier Christian Radio

2002–present Various roles volunteering at St Mary's Church, Reigate

If you want to get in touch about anything in this book, I can be contacted via CWR or at www.andypeck.net

1. Starting out

'Do nothing out of selfish ambition or vain conceit. Rather, in humility value others above yourselves, not looking to your own interests but each of you to the interests of the others.' (Phil. 2:3–4)

It was October 2009, and I was meeting a friend of a friend for lunch in a countryside pub in leafy Surrey. My eating companion was a Christian man in his fifties, involved in charity work local to where I was working, and it was the first time we had met. Knowing that I hosted a radio show on leadership, he asked me whether there were any particular trends in thinking about Christian leadership.

'My guests are from many walks of life, but primarily the Church and charity sectors. They have a range of views, but within the context of wanting to serve Christ where He has placed them,' I replied.

He paused eating and replied, 'Yes, that's what I kind of expected you to say. But who are they really serving as they lead?'

'Well, God,' I said, surprised at the question.

He smiled. 'I am sure they think they are serving God, but I have to be honest. A lot of the church leadership I observe consists in individuals coming up with ideas that they hope will bless God's people, and then doing their best to convince those people that this is the way ahead. They serve themselves, and their egos. In practice, they operate as if God has set things in motion and then gone off on a very long holiday!'

I protested that I didn't think the leaders on my show were like that.

'That's as may be,' he said. 'But don't underestimate the way the power of being a leader affects you. It affects us all. It will probably get me, in the end, if I am not careful.'

He proceeded to share a few stories of his lay leadership in a local Baptist church, and what he believed God had called him to do – which amounted to giving his opponents on a particular issue exactly what they wanted. It was clear he cared deeply about those he was critiquing, a bit like a father might be disappointed that a son hadn't done as well as he could. So although the words themselves might seem harsh, I sensed a gentle, caring tone.

I later asked him, 'Do you really think that most church leaders serve themselves?'

He explained that he'd been sharing with a group of church

leaders locally a few months prior, and someone had written on the board: 'Do not be called leaders; for One is your Leader, *that is*, Christ' (Matt. 23:10, NASB). Discuss.

He had asked the group how many were actually depending on their title to lead, rather than serving others in the way outlined by Jesus. It had gone very quiet, and conversation afterwards suggested this was exactly what many of them were doing.

My lunch companion was not saying, 'There are leaders who are violating a classic command – such as adultery or embezzling money.' That would be obvious. He was asking whether the motives behind their leading were mirroring the world, rather than the Christ they claimed to serve. From my journalism experience I knew charities that had imported business concepts lock, stock and barrel into their operations, without any apparent consideration over what may be regarded as Christian principles. I had seen church leaders bully their members into following their vision. I had seen individuals operating in ways that might have seemed self-promoting rather than God-promoting. I had seen charities seemingly competing with each other, rather than focusing on the kingdom. I was sure he had a point.

Now questioning motives is always a tricky business. Anyone serving in church leadership has put their head above the parapet and tried to make a difference. These leaders have agreed to get involved in leading their church when they could have settled for an 'easier' life, and at that level are to be commended. Sometimes our assumptions tell us more about how *we* might think and feel than the reality of the person we are critiquing. But I know enough of my own heart and struggles to realise that calling yourself Christian doesn't mean what you do is especially Christian.

Our lunchtime discussion that day got me thinking: what does it mean to be a Christian leader? Or, to the point, what kind of leadership does Jesus advocate? How do we lead as God intends us to? I wondered how many Christians were kept from leadership because of what they saw in others. I wondered what it might mean for all Christians to truly lead in a Christlike manner, and the benefit this would be to churches, charities and institutions across our land. And I wondered how much of my own church leadership had been about my own desires to succeed.

A few days later, I phoned my new friend to invite him to share his views on my radio show, figuring that it might shake things up a bit. He declined. 'I think it's wise that I don't have a public profile on saying these things,' he said. So in case you were wondering, this is why I have not named him.

'Christian' leadership?

What actually makes leadership 'Christian' compared to any other kind? How could we make sure we are leading in ways that Jesus commends?

It was Rob Bell (then the pastor of Mars Hill Bible Church in Michigan) who helpfully suggested in his book, *Velvet Elvis*, that '"Christian" makes a great noun and a poor adjective'.[1] He was writing about the idea of a 'Christian band' or 'Christian film', but he could equally have included 'Christian leader'.

Christians lead using skills that, on many levels, are no different from a person using them from any other faith or none – vision casting, strategising, fundraising, teaching, equipping, conflict resolution, and time management. There are wise and foolish ways of doing each. Someone once said to me: 'When someone operates on me, do I want a Christian surgeon, or someone who knows what they are doing?'

So, what makes your way of leading 'Christian'? I would always have figured that it would have to come from the teaching of Jesus. But I was surprised to discover that Jesus mentions leadership directly just twice when training His disciples. If you were basing how Jesus views the topic on how often He spoke of it, you might think it of little importance. But if you look at the teaching of Jesus in the context of what He was doing with the Twelve, you find an altogether different picture. Let me explain.

The kingdom

We sometimes wrench Jesus' life out of His first-century context, and focus on His life, death and resurrection on behalf of the world. Yes, this was vital, but Jesus comes first to His covenant people – those who had received promises from God in Abraham, which were reaffirmed and extended through Moses, and deepened and extended under David. Israel had failed in their role as a kingdom of priests (Exod. 19:6) and light to the nations (Isa. 49:6), and had spent time in Exile (under Assyria and Babylon).[2]

The big question for God's people at the time of Jesus was: how do we live as God's people? The Old Testament scriptures had described God's interventions in the great stories of Moses, Joshua, David and Daniel, but no prophet had spoken for 400 years and these kinds of happenings were absent. The Pharisees had made their version of holiness the key way, the Sadducees had allied themselves with the ruling powers, the Essenes opted for a monastic approach, and many of the people were too focused on earning a daily crust to give it too much thought. Whatever the answer to that question, everyone knew the timetable, which they had discerned from their understanding of the Old Testament. Their lives were lived in what they rather gloomily called 'this present evil age', awaiting the day when the Messiah would return and they would enter 'the age to come' – an age when the glory of Israel would be restored as in the days of David, when the borders of Israel were at their furthest.

Jesus came announcing that we can know God in a fresh way, and that the rule and reign of God (the kingdom of God) could be known through His ministry. This replicated and extended God's works in the Old Testament ushering in a new age to come, *while the present evil age is still continuing*. He also warned the people that if they didn't repent, judgment would come, as big and real as that under the Babylonians who took them into Exile (a judgment that would eventually come in AD 70 with the fall of Jerusalem).

Dallas Willard helpfully summarises the kingdom of God as 'where what God wants done, is done'.[3] It was observed in miracles, healings and even the dead being raised, as God intervened in daily life. The kingdom of God was embraced by faith as people chose to follow in the way of Jesus, turn from sin (living their own way, which leads to death) and embrace His way.

Quite rightly, Jesus' followers slowly began to acknowledge Him as God come to earth, but the fascinating aspect (which is often overlooked) is that He involved them in His work. He commissioned the Twelve to preach, heal and cast out demons in His name. Jesus' provision of supernatural power would accompany them as they travelled and preached. He was giving them signed blank ministry cheques that they could cash as they needed to.

On one level it was a simple franchise arrangement, which Jesus employed to cover more ground in His three years. But it was also part of a two-phase programme Jesus had. Phase one involved His own three-year public ministry culminating in crucifixion, resurrection and ascension. This accomplished God's plan that His own Son would make fellowship with Him gloriously possible, as He ushered in a new era in human affairs. His death was understood to be a once-for-all sacrifice for anyone who put their faith in Him. He was dying for the sins of the world. His resurrection ushers in a new era. A man has come back to life. This changes everything. Put your confidence in Him and you too can know resurrection life.

Phase two involved a different kind of power-sharing arrangement, where the Holy Spirit (described as a being just like Him) would empower His followers to continue His work when He had left this earth.

Jesus' leadership training

As I said earlier, Jesus seemed to say very little about 'leading', as such. We can see that all that Jesus says and does with the Twelve was to be the template for their leading of others – their leadership training programme, if you will. He was changing and subverting what leadership was about. God's kingdom was paramount. He was *the* ruler. But as they learned His way, the disciples learned that leading is not forcing your way, or bullying or pulling rank, but serving others in His name, that God's name and kingdom might be known.

To illustrate, footballing legend Johan Cruyff (pronounced 'Crife') was a hero of mine growing up. It was at a time when England missed qualifying for the World Cup in 1974, so I followed Holland as my team instead. I was mesmerised watching Cruyff play on TV. As a player he had electric pace and stunning technique. Despite being a striker, he would practically run the game. He subsequently went on to coach and manage, incorporating many of the methods that had made the Holland team famous. His methods were popular, and his main tactic placed an emphasis on keeping possession of the ball, and pressing the opponents high up the pitch when possession was lost. It was a totally fresh approach. Some of the best in the business today have learnt what they know from Cruyff.

But you couldn't claim to be a disciple of Cruyff if you adopted different tactics to him. You could claim to have watched recordings of his old matches, or listened to him explain his approach. You might even spend time with coaches that like him. But the only measure that truly counts is: do you do what he did?

Here's where I believe my lunch buddy was correct in his assertions. Plenty of people claim to be Christians in their leading of churches, but even being charitable, you have to question whether they are seeking to influence others towards godly purposes in the manner Jesus taught. It might be that they had not understood what following Jesus was about, perhaps because they were early in the journey. Or maybe they had understood it, but were ignoring what

He said. Either way, they may claim to be Christian leaders, but leadership that is truly 'Christian' is conducted by those who are imitating Christ.

When we invite someone to put their trust in Jesus, it's typically because we have stressed the benefits of forgiveness of sin and relationship with God, which begins now and continues into the life to come. However, we have often failed to mention that we are inviting them into a leadership training programme – which involves the character transformation aspect and all that Jesus taught His followers to do – in announcing and demonstrating that kingdom.

We see 'phase two' being worked out in the book of Acts, as the apostles preached this good news of the rule of God and all Jesus had accomplished. Their message was that God had raised Jesus from the dead, so a new reality exists that changes everything. *You too can know forgiveness of sins and the life of the kingdom.* And the apostles demonstrated that very same kingdom. Indeed – in Antioch, the sneering nickname of Christian ('belong to Christ', or 'little Christs') was a back-handed compliment, in that the way they were living sought to imitate their Master.

What does leading look like?

The whole of Jesus' teaching therefore sums up the way Jesus calls us to lead. But the two passages where Jesus specifically mentions leading in the context of the Twelve give us a key motif. They are both in Matthew's Gospel (and in one case parallel passages in the other Gospels). They may be only two passages, and they may not say all we need to learn, but they are helpful to our theme.

> 'You know that the rulers of the Gentiles lord it over
> them, and their high officials exercise authority over
> them. Not so with you. Instead, whoever wants to
> become great among you must be your servant, and

whoever wants to be first must be your slave – just as
the Son of Man did not come to be served, but to serve,
and to give his life as a ransom for many.'
(Matt. 20:25–28; see also Mark 10:42–45,
Luke 22:25–26)

The second is the passage my friend quoted earlier and is in the context of the Pharisees and teachers of the Law (the religious leaders), who liked the title 'Rabbi' because it made them feel good:

'The greatest among you will be your servant. For those
who exalt themselves will be humbled, and those who
humble themselves will be exalted.' (Matt. 23:11–12)

You don't need a degree in theology to spot that *serving others* is the key theme for each. Jesus' followers were to lead differently to the approach of the Jewish and Gentile worlds, both of which tended to have leaders who ordered people around. Jesus was saying there is a fundamentally different way of seeing life when you acknowledge that God runs the show and has sent His Son, to whom all authority will be given (Matt. 28:18).

The Greek words for service, *diakonos* and *doulos* ('servant' and 'slave') are at the very bottom of the social ladder, and this was radical thinking. No one valued service and humility. It's worth considering what Jesus meant by the metaphor of a slave. Serving others means serving according to the ultimate good of those being served. In that sense, it is not the service of a slave bound to do their master's bidding, but serving our heavenly Master.

Jesus exercises many roles as a leader, even though He sees Himself as 'servant of all'. At times He is forceful and persuasive. He is frank and uncompromising. He charms and rebukes. He amuses and He condemns. But here's the main thing: He does not employ force. Just as His Father sets up a universe with human beings who can shake their fist at Him and write books claiming He doesn't exist, Jesus loves everyone, holds out His hand to all, offers everything – but lets us *choose*. His was a different way that overturned the leadership norms of His day and ours. Leading was serving others, not being overbearing. Leading was joining with the Father in what He was doing, not cooking up clever ideas by Himself. Leading was knowing the easy yoke of peace and joy, not the struggle of pain and strife. Leading was joyfully entering into all that our destiny as image bearers entails, with the smile of the Father upon us, knowing that we can bring goodness and life into places of pain and despair.

Servant leadership doesn't mean we will always lead according to what our 'followers' want. We serve Jesus when we speak powerfully, argue our point convincingly and call people to act according to their best motives, even if they don't like what we say. But it does mean we don't serve according to what we 'want', as if others are there to serve us.

Consider this: Jesus has risen from the dead and is proclaimed Lord of all. This is the greatest event in the history of the world. We would henceforth see life in terms of BC and AD (in the year of our Lord), so life-changing it is. As far as Jesus was concerned, the leadership training of the Twelve and the coming of the Spirit was all that was necessary for God's restoration programme to continue. He would carry on leading His people by His Spirit, as they invited Him and involved Him in the task. Thus, in instructing the Twelve about leading others in these passages and in all His teaching, Jesus doesn't feel the need to be prescriptive, trusting that as their characters are developed and empowered by the Spirit (who will come at Pentecost), they will know *how* to lead whoever and whatever they lead in the future.

In a sense, there is no one way. People who claim a 'biblical way' or a 'Christian way' need to understand the nuances of each leadership role. Christians serve as heads of state and as school caretakers, as CEOs of Fortune 500 companies and as heads of the PTA, as pastors of churches and as leaders of university departments, as heads of taxi firms and partners in law firms, as heads of families and heads of supermarkets. Each is called to read and immerse themselves in the teaching of Jesus and welcome His Spirit so that they can lead in the 'Jesus way' – whether or not this is obvious to those they lead, however counter-cultural this may seem and however lonely they feel in the task. And as they are called to lead, they do so as a disciple of Jesus, conscious that He has commissioned them to help others to be followers too.

Anyone looking to work out what matters to Jesus need look no further than His teaching in the Gospels – and it's not as much reading as you might think (you can read the shortest, Mark, in a couple of hours). This is our curriculum. There are plenty of books on leadership and related topics, but our first priority should be to focus on Jesus' curriculum from the Gospels, and allow the Holy Spirit to inspire and instruct us in the particular role or roles in which we find ourselves. It is this narrow focus that I want to explore more throughout this book.

The leadership road less travelled

Leading in the way of Jesus by the power of the Spirit is the road 'less travelled', partly because it is not understood, partly because it requires humility on our part, and partly because it matters so much that we will be opposed as we try and walk it – because just as soon as God's people do start walking it, real changes can unfold in our spheres of influence. It's the road that will transform our churches, our communities and our cities. It's the way that we can invite others into, that we can teach to our families, that we can drop into conversation with those we know.

Of course, you will need to get the best training you can to lead whatever it is you lead. You will benefit from books that explore the issues where you are weak. You will have mentors and coaches that can help you. Leadership skills are universally required, whether you have a faith or not. But if you want to walk the leadership road less travelled, it will be as you lead from who you are as a person who is learning the way of Jesus by the power of the Spirit.

I hope to convince you that this is the only way for a Christian to lead, and to help you discover how to maintain that kind of focus in your leadership. But first, let's focus on the all-important question: if this is the leadership road less travelled, leading the way God intends me to, how do I go about it?

....

Questions to consider

- How do you imagine Jesus leading others?
- Does the analysis that church and charity leaders might be leading from ego seem harsh to you, or accurate?
- How do you respond to the idea of the leadership road less travelled as you start this book?

2. Modelling it

'The student is not above the teacher, but everyone who is fully trained will be like their teacher.' (Luke 6:40)

I had driven to a leisure centre in Eastleigh, Hampshire, a few miles from where I worked in Southampton. I was listening to a talk by John Ortberg on cassette tape (remember those?!). As I parked the car, his talk had reached the point where he was urging church leaders to call people to live the life they were living:

'Don't just tell them what they must do, but model it.'

The words hit me deep in my guts. Could I actually call those in the church I served to live the life I was living? I could call them to lead the life I believed the Bible taught, but to what extent could I say to them (as the apostle Paul could), 'follow me as I follow Christ'?

The issue is not an uncommon one for anyone who is a Christian leader. We all face the challenge of practising what we preach. We know what the gospel says and how we should live, but we are people 'in process'. Ortberg's challenging words set me on a journey. I discovered that he had benefited from a writer and mentor, Dallas Willard, a former Baptist pastor. Willard put his finger on something that to my shame I had never grasped: 'We cannot by direct effort do what Christ commands but we can become the kind of people who naturally do what Christ commands.'[1]

It was this principle that transformed my understanding of the Christian life and Christian leadership. If leading 'Christianly' is done in the way of Jesus, how can I lead like Him?

Like many in the evangelical framework, I was very faithful in the practices of Bible reading, prayer and corporate worship. I had been taught the value of the 'daily quiet time' and, being a disciplined sort of guy, I'd make sure I spent time doing something. I thank God for His grace towards me through this, and what follows is not intended to minimise their value. But what I hadn't fully realised is that these were just *some* of the practices we are called to adopt, and that there are deeper and fresher experiences of God to be known and felt. Jesus did certain things to be the Person He was. You might argue that as the Son of God He had a head-start, and I don't presume to comprehend fully how He can be simultaneously God and man. But

I equally believe that, in His humanity, He needed to ensure that He had a smooth, unbroken connection with His Father through the Holy Spirit, who had come upon Him at His baptism. It was this that sustained Jesus in His leading, and is the leadership road that He invites us to join Him on.

If you are a leader, can I ask you to consider your average week? Your activities, when and where you travel, who you meet with, who you speak with, what your desired outcomes are…

I would argue that everything we do can be part of what the apostle Paul wrote about in Colossians 3:17. After outlining the new life in Christ, he says:

> 'Let every detail in your lives—words, actions,
> whatever—be done in the name of the Master, Jesus,
> thanking God the Father every step of the way.'
> (The Message)

Chatting to admin staff, conducting appraisals, calling customers, preparing talks, browsing online, texting a friend… these are all part of the 'whatever'!

But how might you follow the command to do it in the name of Jesus when the client is irritating, when the audience is hostile, when your colleague is unpleasant? You might fake it, or have the composure to do the right thing, but the leading in the way of Christ – by the power of Christ – comes more naturally as you routinely live in an attitude of love and grace and forgiveness. For that to happen, God has to be at work in you before you ever enter the public arena. This is the equivalent of the gym training behind an athlete's performance on the track. Jesus says: 'apart from me you can do nothing' (John 15:5) – and that certainly includes leading His way.

Again, Dallas Willard provides a helpful framework for understanding how we typically nurture our inner life, using the acronym 'VIM' (Vision, Intention, Means).[2]

Vision

For any change to happen, we need to have a vision for the future – whether this be of a violin played perfectly, a language spoken fluently, a golf course mastered, or a perfectly toned six-pack (sadly I can't manage any of these).

It's the same for the leadership road less travelled, walking in the way of Christ in the power of the Spirit. You need to have a vision for what that looks like if change is to occur. For many, vision is developed through reflection on Scripture and how the first followers lived in the kingdom (have a look at the book of Acts and see how the believers turned the world upside down). Others are inspired by stories. Vision of what leadership can accomplish is also important, but not our concern here. This is vision of you living as a leader, leading in ways that honour Christ.

Intention

Vision needs to lead to intention. If it doesn't, we obviously haven't been impressed enough with the value of change. Many would like a different future, but few act accordingly – which is why this book has 'less travelled' in the title. God Himself will be willing us to do good things, but you will need to *decide* to change. It won't just happen to you by some kind of osmosis within a church environment. You need to want to change, or at least *want to* want to change.

Means

And then the means. Some call them 'spiritual disciplines' (though the word 'discipline' may have unhelpful connotations). Some prefer 'habits' (perhaps not the best word either, given that habits can be good and bad). The word 'spiritual' in both these descriptions can be understood today, by some, as simply unseen and mystical.

I like the wording 'practices in the way of Jesus' because it reminds us why we are doing what we're doing. Willard uses the word 'means' (sometimes lengthened to 'means of grace') because they are activities we engage in, through which the grace of God is at work.

Think about it like this. When you eat, you have to select, chew and swallow your food. But you do nothing to actually ensure that your body draws the correct nutrients from the food for the energy it needs. This happens automatically as parts of your body, beyond your conscious awareness, do their vital work. In the same way, we read, listen, pray, etc – but the benefit comes as God (who we cannot control but in whom we trust) works within us to change us from the inside out.

You may find that your capacity to change is limited or impaired, and needs someone to ease the process for you. Perhaps you have made unwise choices in the past that make it hard for you to co-operate with what the Spirit is doing, and one-to-one conversations with someone experienced (or some more in-depth counselling) may be required.

In his introductory essay for *The Spiritual Formation Bible*, Richard Foster says:

> 'We cannot by direct effort make ourselves into the kind of people who can live fully alive to God. Only God can accomplish this in us... We do not, for example, become humble merely by trying to become humble. Action on our own would make us all the more proud of our humility. No, we instead train with Spiritual Disciplines appropriate to our need... By an act of the will we choose to take up disciplines of the spiritual life that we can do. These disciplines are all actions of body, mind, and spirit that are within our power to do... Then the grace of God steps in, takes this simple offering of ourselves, and creates out of it the kind of person who embodies the goodness of God.'[3]

At no point in the Gospels does Jesus list a series of key activities that He insists His followers *must* complete. Instead, we have the assumption by Jesus that His followers, as those part of the covenant people of God, will practise their faith in the normal way – which included learning Torah (the Law), praying and fasting, fulfilling the annual feast days etc. For example, He says, *'when* you pray' (Matt 6:6, emphasis added) and *'when* you fast' (Matt 6:16, emphasis added). The fact that He says 'when' and not 'if' seems to assume that these would be the practices of the hearers. As those under the new covenant, we don't learn Torah (the Law) in the same way, thankful that Jesus fulfilled it perfectly, but there are many other practices that Jesus undertakes in the Gospels:

Prayer – We read that Jesus went up to the hills to pray (Mark 1:35; John 17).

Solitude – Jesus would take Himself away from any human contact (Mark 1:35; 6:32; Luke 4:42; 9:10).

Fasting – This is when we voluntarily go without something (often food) for a period in order to present ourselves to God (see Matt. 4:1–11 and Jesus' instruction in Matt. 6:16).

Study – It is clear that Jesus spent concerted time focusing on God's Word, as evident in His grasp and ability to quote from the Old Testament (Matt. 22:42–46).

Meditation – Mulling over the Word of God, often involving memorising key phrases. All Jewish boys memorised Scripture, and Jesus is no exception.

Submission – Jesus gave His life in ministry, not just on the cross (John 13:1–11).

Worship – Jesus attended the synagogue, the Temple and regular festivals of the Jewish people (Matt. 11:25–26; John 7:10). Our worship will be the conscious living of all of life in praise to God, including praise in word and song with other Christians.

Celebration – As one participating in the feasts, Jesus would have probably laughed and danced with everyone, as they enjoyed the food and celebrations prescribed.

Sabbath – Taking a day off from work and regular routines for worship, rest and recuperation. This was a Saturday for Jesus, typically a Sunday for most Christians, though it could be any day of the week.

Of course, most books add the discipline of confession, which Jesus didn't need to practise. But John reminds us that, 'if we confess our sins, he is faithful and just to forgive us our sins and purify us from all unrighteousness' (1 John 1:9). What a wonderful thing to be able to begin each day knowing we have no barrier with the living God!

It's important to underline again that the truth of the gospel is that we are accepted through Christ on the basis of our faith. Daily confidence in Christ leads us to look to Him, which will include living the kind of life He lived. This is not Christianity by works, but Christianity that responds to the goodness of God in Christ, and puts us in the way of God's Spirit.

Now you may be thinking, *yikes… how am I going to have time for all this?*

I suggest you look through and decide which activities will be daily, weekly, fortnightly and so on. For example:

Daily – prayer and Bible study, 20 minutes.

Weekly – engaging with other Christians in worship; study with other Christians and alone; Sabbath rest.

Fortnightly – fast (miss breakfast and lunch); spend two hours in solitude and silence.

Monthly – celebration; have Christian friends around for a meal to share news and celebrate all God is doing.

Occasionally – submission; spend a day when, where possible, you submit to the wills of those around you.

At any given time, some of the practices may be especially precious to you. If you are in the limelight and things are going well, you may especially need the times of solitude and silence. When facing particular temptation, especially around sexual desire, fasting can be especially beneficial. Those leading in environments that are hostile to the Christian faith will benefit especially from worship and celebration.

It's worth saying, too, that a little help on practising these approaches may be needed. Bible study can be dull or dynamic depending on which books you read alongside it. I recommend using daily Bible reading notes that work for you. (If you're not sure where to start, CWR produce these for all ages and levels of faith.) You might benefit from Tom Wright's *New Testament for Everyone* series, and the guides that go with it. And as we saw in the last chapter, reading the Gospels will be key to our curriculum for leading as Jesus taught His first followers. Prayer is absolutely vital, but you may need reminders of the range of types of praying, and how God works.[4]

Is it possible to be a Christian leader without these practices? Well, a mature believer might manage for a while in a season where they are extremely busy. But Jesus notably practises them all! Indeed, at times when He is especially busy and successful, He makes it a priority to get away and spend time alone in prayer. In Matthew 14 (and elsewhere in all four Gospels) we read that He miraculously feeds 5,000 with five loaves and two fish. But rather than bask in the 'glory' or success, we read that He sends His disciples on ahead, and goes into the hills to pray.

We don't know how often Jesus did what, and I would hate for you to pick up any legalism in what I am writing. But such is the potential power of practising the ways of Jesus, and the transformation to your leadership, that I am fairly sure you will find it something of a battle to actually do what I have suggested. Habits are tough to change in any case, and especially ones that have a spiritual dimension. Don't be surprised if you find some road blocks and diversions in the journey at this point – you may find it's a case of three steps forward, two steps back, before you make steady progress. Persevere and you will find the blessings the other side of using these means of grace make it all well worth it.

The leadership road less travelled will vary enormously according to the kind of leading you engage in. Those leading a family will apply the approach differently to those leading a small group or a church. Those leading a business will be different from those leading a sports team.

You may not see immediate benefits, but as you read and pray and listen and worship, bit by bit, God will meet with you and you will change. It's what God does. He is committed to your growth. It's His business. He's been at it a long time, and He has worked with more stubborn and uncooperative people than you. These are the crucial vital first steps because they are the ones that help put your hand in God's as He leads you.

And the beauty is that as you diligently put growth in God at the very heart of your life – and therefore your leadership – you will know that you have put first things first. You have done all you can to place yourself in the blessing of God. You can relax and trust Him. This won't mean you won't get abuse, criticism, slander or opposition, but it will mean that if and when it comes, you will be well placed to overcome it.

In the course of hosting *The Leadership File*, I have had the privilege of meeting many men and women who were walking this road, including Dallas Willard, mentioned earlier. Their responsibilities were huge and the concerns could have been overwhelming, but they would gently speak of the goodness of God, their confidence in Him to lead what they were involved in, and their joy that they got to be part of it. My thanks to all who have showed me the way and inspired me to make good steps myself.

Questions to consider

- How many of the practices of Jesus have you tried?
- Which will you do first?
- Have you had evidence of God meeting with you and equipping you through any of these practices?

3. Keep your ID on you

'To them God has chosen to make known among the Gentiles the glorious riches of this mystery, which is Christ in you, the hope of glory.' (Col. 1:27)

I was shaking hands at the church door after preaching. I was serving as Assistant Pastor at Lansdowne Baptist Church, Bournemouth. It was a lovely place to preach, though at the time the building was Victorian-style with pews downstairs and up, and a little daunting with the upstairs congregation looking down on you as you preached! As an 'assistant' and therefore technically 'learning', I was allowed a monthly slot preaching, pulpit time being divided between the senior pastor, who had the lion's share, and the associate pastor and me. I was growing in confidence, and was feeling quite comfortable with how my sermon that day had gone. Comments on the door had included: 'thank you', 'nice sermon' and the rather more patronising, 'you're coming on…' I was starting to relax when two sisters approached. They were formidable women and had been members of the church for decades. I'd guess that they were in their early seventies.

'Thank you for your sermon. It was, mostly, really good. Have you ever considered having elocution lessons?'

Ouch.

They meant well, but there are times and places for such advice – and the preacher is never more vulnerable than immediately after a service. I tried to smile, but was secretly wondering what planet they were on.

I replied in the calmest voice I could muster: 'As it happens, a woman in the church who tutors in breathing exercises for singers has agreed to see me, as she has noticed that my breathing could be improved. So I am receiving help, but thanks anyway!'

Let me add that the people at Lansdowne were wonderfully welcoming and it was an enormous privilege to have served there, but I'll always remember that comment and the bruise it left on my ego.

The role of the ego in leading is a well-trodden theme in Christian literature and you won't be unaware of its significance. It's an enormously tricky area to comment on given that the development of the ego and its place in our personality is massively complex, and what may be my issues in this area, may not be yours. We are in an era of self-promotion, and it is often hard to assess whether someone is blowing their own trumpet or God's, when they proclaim the good things God has done. As we noted in the first chapter, it is dangerous to believe we can assess the motivations of others, knowing it may say more about how we might be if we were in their shoes.

But if you are in leadership or aspire to be, you will need to grasp a firm understanding of self in the context of your walk with Christ if you are to resist the pressure that will come your way. You will need to be robust enough to withstand those keen to shoot you down, but humble enough to recognise that you are a work in progress.

Here are some tips on having a correct view of self as you lead.

1. You're just doing what you are designed for!

At the very beginning of the Bible, we read what human beings were created for:

> 'Then God said, "Let us make mankind in our image,
> in our likeness, so that they may rule over the fish in
> the sea and the birds in the sky, over the livestock and
> all the wild animals,and over all the creatures that
> move along the ground."
> So God created mankind in his own image,
> in the image of God he created them;
> male and female he created them.
> God blessed them and said to them, "Be fruitful and
> increase in number; fill the earth and subdue it. Rule
> over the fish in the sea and the birds in the sky and over
> every living creature that moves on the ground."'
> (Gen. 1:26–28)

Scholars have speculated on what is meant by 'image of God', but the context is clear that 'ruling' is a key element. The text can be translated, 'God made humans in order to rule'. The Hebrew word for 'rule' implies kingly language. Later, we read we are to 'fill the earth and subdue' – a reference to procreation, but also to the fact that the earth itself would need some form of ruling over. The implication is that we have been made with an instinct to have mastery over our surroundings, to bring order out of chaos. One Hebrew scholar translated it as 'to actively partner with God in taking the world somewhere.'

Of course, sin exists within humanity from Genesis 3, when Adam and Eve rebel against their maker. And though it is clear that a spiritual death occurs at this point (the penalty God had promised if they ate of the forbidden fruit), we are not told that humanity ceases to be image bearers. Indeed in Genesis 9, after the Flood, Noah receives a similar blessing to the one given Adam, and the reminder that humans are still made 'in the image of God' (Gen. 9:6).

What is a chair for? It is furniture to sit on. What is a lamp for? To give light to a dark room. What is a human being for? To be a co-ruler with God! When we lead, we are fulfilling our purpose. When I first discovered this, it was revolutionary. In my late teens and early twenties, I had been troubled by the question, 'am I called to be a pastor?' When things unravelled and I no longer sought a pastoral positon, I wondered whether I had somehow denied my calling. This text tells me that leadership is intrinsic to being human, despite the fact that we so often put it on a pedestal. It doesn't tell me whether being a pastor was a good idea or not, but it affirms that my leadership instincts are good.

You might be reading this because you are a leader or aspire to be one. You have been made to rule. In the course of this book I want to encourage you to encourage others to step into their God-given role. There are plenty of people ruling according to their own preferences – how much better to have people ruling who work with God? Think what a difference the body of Christ could make if it really grasped this.

I had been hosting the radio show on Premier for over ten years before anyone ever articulated anything like this idea. Then I hosted Trevor Waldock, who had swapped coaching stockbrokers and CEOs to become the founding director of Emerging Leaders, which has provided leadership training free to young people in some of the poorest nations in the world. In the course of our interview, he stated enthusiastically on air:

'I believe everyone is a leader at some level of their lives.'

'Everyone?' I asked.

'Yes, everyone.'

By then, Emerging Leaders had trained thousands of young people in various countries across Africa in leadership principles, on the understanding that those who benefitted would teach ten other people. I asked whether they had ever screened anyone.

'No!'

'Not even those with mental health issues?'

'Well, it depends what you mean by "health" issues. But no, anyone is free to come if they want to,' Trevor confirmed.

Everyone is a leader? Really? Well, at some level. If humans are created as co-rulers with God, is it not likely that many will do what they have been created for, even if many don't have a God framework for what they do?

Trevor went on to quote Howard Gardner, author of *Leading Minds*. He defines a leader thus: 'A leader is an individual (or, rarely, a set of individuals) who creates a story that affects the thoughts, feelings, and/or behaviours of a significant number of individuals.'[1] The story he has in mind concerns a narrative way of looking at reality. The leader describes the past, present and future, and invites others to create the story together, based on a vision of a preferred future. Trevor's charity, Emerging Leaders, uses the metaphor of the pen. We all have a blank page in our future. What future are we going to write?

This kind of understanding helps us remember that leaders are not a breed apart, even if some are clearly doing extraordinary things. At one level, as you lead, you are merely being human.

2. Be clear on your identity

I have been slow to learn that my identity in Christ is the key to not allowing any criticism or brickbats to sink me. In the past, I could be taken out emotionally for days at a time by a callous remark or a questioning of motive. Knowing the truth theologically is one thing, but the journey from brain to heart is not always a smooth one.

Knowing who we are in Christ is vital when it comes to having an inner peace while serving as a leader. When I came to record my six-hundredth show for *The Leadership File,* I wanted to find a guest who would be a little different – as a kind of celebration. I discovered through a mutual friend that Leif Hetland (of Global Mission Awareness) would be in Winchester, so I put in a request to interview him and was able to secure a half-hour slot. Leif (pronounced 'Lafe') was a Norwegian evangelist living in Atlanta, who had seen half a million people come to faith by the year 2000. He had visited over fifty nations with the gospel. But, as he described in an interview with me, he was like the elder son in the parable of the prodigal son – slaving in the fields, not really knowing the home that his Father provided. You will recall that the focus of this parable (see Luke 15:11) is often on the younger son – the prodigal – who is restored to his father as a son, despite his apparently 'unforgivable' rebellion and disrespect. But the older son, having never strayed from home, hears the rejoicing over the younger son's return, but is outraged by how unjust he sees it to be. He complains to the father for having been such a good son and never enjoying such lavish attention. Perhaps the key to the parable lies in the words of the father:

> *"'My son,' the father said, 'you are always with me, and* everything I have is yours. *But we had to celebrate and*

be glad, because this brother of yours was dead and is
alive again; he was lost and is found.'" (Luke 15:31–32,
emphasis added)

Leif explained that we can so often behave like the older son. Looking
back, I worked seriously hard: evenings, early mornings, weekends. It
was as if I was slaving to please my heavenly Father and the Church
He oversaw. But did I have what Leif calls an 'orphan heart' that
didn't know the love of the father, seeking His approval in sermons
preached, doors knocked on, people cared for? I'm not sure – but as
Leif spoke, it rang a few bells.

The message of the gospel is that *all God has* is yours in Christ! You
don't work *for* approval but *from* approval. You are blessed that you
may be a blessing. You give to others what you have received. This is
the logic and the economy of God's kingdom.

In Leif Hetland's case, it was through a special encounter with the
love of God the Father that he came into an understanding that we
live from God, not for God. He continues to see many come to faith,
but from a totally different motivation. As he said: 'You don't see the
world the way it is, but the way you are.'

3. Keep following Jesus central

Knowing our security as a loved child of God, adopted into His family,
becomes the foundation for our pursuit of spiritual growth. If we
really grasp the goodness of God and see Him at work, it's hard to be
too proud! In the world of football we have the frequent spectacle of
a goal scorer running to bask in the adulation of the crowd, pointing
to their name printed on the back of their shirt – when all they had
done was tap the ball over the line following a passing movement
involving six other players.

In Acts 3, following the miraculous healing of a lame man, Peter
asks, 'Why do you stare at us as if by our own power or godliness we

had made this man walk?' (Acts 3:12). Yet Christian leaders have been quite happy to be stared at for things they have done, as if it was down to them.

When we realise we are part of something bigger and better than us, which our ingenuity cannot manufacture, I hope we are duly modest if we have had a hand in success.

When the apostles are beaten for their faith, Scripture says that they were grateful to be 'counted worthy of suffering disgrace' (Acts 5:41). Early Church tradition suggests that most of the apostles were martyred for their faith, and some accounts suggest the joy they felt as they followed the way of their Master.[2] Peter (himself martyred, according to these same accounts) says in his first epistle: 'God opposes the proud but shows favour to the humble' (1 Pet. 5:5). Who wants to be opposed by Almighty God?

4. Be humbly grateful for how things are

At one level, leadership is all about you. Your CV lists *your* accomplishments, after all. A prospective employer is looking at your track record, accomplishments, references to character – and in that sense, you can't get away from it being about you. But there's a leap between acknowledging your strengths and being inappropriately proud of them. The apostle Paul encourages us not to think of ourselves 'more highly than you ought' but with 'sober judgment' (Rom. 12:3). Should the CEO expect adoration from shareholders as they see the end of year accounts and point to his name badge as they applaud his contribution?!

Thankfully, I came across a precious verse early in my career:

> *'What do you have that you did not receive? And if you did receive it, why do you boast as though you did not?'*
> (1 Cor. 4:7).

If you are a fine leader, good with figures, a brilliant raconteur, fantastic listener, strategic thinker – thank God! Be pleased that you are, and even thank people who thank you. But don't harbour inappropriate pride. Be humbly grateful.

Maybe you've heard of the preacher shaking hands with his congregation as they left after the service. An elderly gentleman thanked him for his excellent talk.

'It wasn't me,' said the preacher, 'it was the Holy Spirit.'

The gentleman paused before replying.

'Well, it was a cracking talk... but it wasn't that good!'

5. Rejoice in what God is doing in you

In my early days of hosting *The Leadership File* I had the privilege of interviewing a hairy Australian by the name of Fuzz Kitto (yes – a great name!). He was a youth worker, and was in the UK speaking at a conference. His ministry involved helping churches with their missional focus locally, and he explained how he went about working with churches.

'First, I ask the leaders where they believe God is? If they say, "in the church", or "in His Word", I know where the problem lies,' he explained.

According to Fuzz, God is at work in the world drawing people to Himself, as well as the two places they might have mentioned.

His question has stuck with me, and is one we can usefully ask when it comes to our lives. So, I ask you now: where is God, primarily, for you? Your answer may tell you a lot about potential ego problems. Is He up in heaven looking down on you? Is He within you by His Spirit? Do you see him as Christ in the pages of Scripture?

Bill Johnson (the senior pastor of Bethel Church, Redding, California) caricatures the Christian who has what he calls 'worm theology'. He typically prays: 'None of me and all of you, Lord!' To which God replies, 'I had none of you before, that's why I made you!'

We have a sinful self that was crucified with Christ when we came to faith. At times we keep it on life support, and we see its ugliness. But we don't want any of that. It's not about us – so in that sense we do pray, 'none of that, Lord!' But Paul writes to the Colossians: 'Christ in you, the hope of glory' (Col. 1:27). Don't we want some of that?

Here's the paradox at the heart of the Christian life; the great exchange, if you will:

> *'God made him who had no sin to be sin for us, so that*
> *in him we might become the righteousness of God.'*
> (2 Cor. 5:21)

So – where is God? He is at work in our world by His Spirit and like Jesus Himself says, we are wise to see what He is doing and partner with Him. Our identity has to be rooted in the love of the Father and in the imitation of the Christ who lives within us. That's the truth – you have Jesus living within you by His Spirit, and He is looking to so permeate your personality and outlook that you are moved to live as Jesus did in love for others. So rejoice in this, and be involved in influencing others for good! If Christ is in you, you don't want to be hiding Him under a bushel. The apostles didn't spread the gospel by staying at home and singing choruses.

Where you lead needs God. God encourages you to be the best, brightest and most hope-filled person in your church, charity, company, family, neighbourhood and leisure activity. Be quick to give Him praise.

6. Keep your eyes on the cause

In a later chapter we will look at the whole topic of how to focus on what God has called you to do, but it's worth considering this under the topic of your identity specifically.

If I am asked to describe my worst experience as a 'Christian worker', it would hands-down be hosting the morning Bible readings on the main stage at Spring Harvest (Minehead) in 2011. The deal is that if you are invited to be part of the Spring Harvest team, you are theoretically available for any task that they may have for you. So having said, 'Sure – sign me up!', I later discovered that I was being asked to lead a workshop on reading and understanding Scripture after the main Bible readings (fine, excited by that); lead a seminar for potential students (great, sounds fun); and host the Bible readings for Andy Hickford in the big top. What...?!

It wasn't that there would be 3,000 people there, nor the fact that Andy was speaking. He was a delight – great fun to host, and I knew him from Bible College days. I was just convinced that I wasn't a good fit; that I didn't match the Spring Harvester profile. I didn't sleep at all the night before kick-off, tossing and turning in the chalet, trying to leave it with God but still feeling stomach-churning terror. In truth I was totally self-conscious, aware that I wasn't the man for the job in any shape or form, not wanting to let Spring Harvest down or be a lousy warm-up for the main man. But somehow, I got through the week without embarrassing myself. And somehow I flexed to deal with the last-minute changes to the programme (every single day). As it turns out, no one died. My family loved the week, and the impact of Spring Harvest on the body of Christ is extraordinary. It was a privilege to be a part of it. Why had I felt so traumatised?

The lesson I learned is this: when you feel self-conscious, focus on the outcomes. The 3,000 people in the big top were not there to hear me. I had 15 minutes – maximum – and much of it was the notices, and introducing video clips. The whole point of the slot was to settle people down, ready for the main teaching. And so now – when I get the nerves before a talk, preach or lead a training day – I focus on what I am hoping God will do, and I become less conscious of how I seem and what I portray, and more hopeful that God is graciously working it all out behind the scenes. Focus on the cause, and somehow your self-consciousness will evaporate.

Of course it's a lifelong challenge, getting out of the way in order to see God at work. But it's important that we stay alive to the need. Paul could say:

> *'I have been crucified with Christ and I no longer live,*
> *but Christ lives in me. The life I now live in the body,*
> *I live by faith in the Son of God, who loved me and gave*
> *himself for me.'* (Gal. 2:20)

We may feel we have a long way to go before we can say that, but that's the aim: to so lose ourselves that Christ's ways are more perfectly seen.

7. Be real about the struggles

If your identity is rooted in your activity, success in any area of leadership can have an incommensurate effect upon you. One radio guest was very candid in his observation of his own ego. He recalled a time when he took time out from leadership to study for a master's degree. Having stepped aside from his leadership to become 'just another student', he talked about a moment when he had really wanted to shout to his peers: 'Don't you know who I am?!'

That guest said many other things during our interview, but it was his candour and honesty that struck me. People will be impressed by your strengths, but are drawn to you by your failures. Will van der Hart (a pastoral chaplain at Holy Trinity Brompton, London) was similarly honest when he said to me: 'Every leader faces imposter syndrome – the feeling that one day you are going to be found out!'

So many of us are insecure. We foolishly assume that we are the only ones facing the problems we face or the hang-ups we encounter. It's why the observational humour of stand-up comedians is often so poignant – they laugh at what we know to be true, speaking aloud what we think in our heads but are frightened to voice. And it's so easy in the 'Christian world' to assume that everyone is on a higher spiritual plane than we are, seeing God work wonderfully because *they* are wonderful. It's as if we haven't understood grace at all.

The friend I mentioned in chapter one had said that he thought that power might get him in the end. He stepped down from leading his charity a few years ago, before it had the chance to. Sadly, many leaders fail to have his wisdom. We are made as rulers, but co-rulers with God. When we allow our identity to be solely in our work or our ministry, we fail to live from Christ and the glorious resources He has. One of Jesus' key leadership lessons to His followers came when James and John asked about their position in the future kingdom. Like those early disciples, we can become so concerned about our position in the kingdom that we completely miss the point.

The leadership road less travelled is to take a healthy view of self. Yes – we matter, we lead and we have been equipped to do so. But we lead knowing that we belong to the one who was rich but became poor, so that we, through His poverty, might become rich.

There's a model to emulate.

....

Questions to consider
- Who are you, really?
- If you lost your title, how would you feel?
- Are you the same person in private as in public? What's different? Is that healthy?

4. Energy for the journey

'Remain in me, as I also remain in you. No branch can bear fruit by itself; it must remain in the vine. Neither can you bear fruit unless you remain in me.'
(John 15:4)

If I am ever asked to name a book that changed my life, I immediately say *The Divine Conspiracy* by Dallas Willard.[1] I read it at just the right time. Eight years of Christian ministry was taking its toll, and I was stepping back for a breather before looking to God for the next step.

I shared in the introduction how I had moved from a full-time pastoral ministry role in my 'dream ministry job'. It was in this period of pushing doors that I read Willard's book, and I devoured it like a a gourmet meal. After the first chapter I decided to ration myself to a few pages a day because I was afraid I would finish it too quickly. The book explored the Sermon on the Mount – a thrilling insight into how Jesus intended human beings to grasp what life is about and how God's kingdom is to be understood. I realised that my grasp of the gospel had been truncated. I had first trusted Jesus when I was seven years of age, and over time had become excited about having a role in seeing others come to faith, particularly when involved with the Christian union at university. We saw 20 come to faith (in a CU of 40) and I headed for Bible College thinking I might one day be in pastoral ministry. But through my time at university, and working in student ministry, I hadn't appreciated that Jesus' message was not 'trust my death', but 'live in the good of the kingdom' (which of course takes care of death). I had failed to appreciate that His yoke really is easy and His burden really is light. As a leader, I didn't have to make things happen, or galvanise people into doing what they didn't want to do. Instead, I was to invite them to enjoy the kingdom too. The pressure was off.

I began to wonder whether my life as a pastor could have known more power because I didn't correctly access the energy that I needed. God had told me to move on because He knew I couldn't keep ploughing the same furrow. I needed fresh understanding.

You can lead without the Holy Spirit and make a passable job at it. But the leadership road less travelled is leading in the way of Christ, by the power of the Spirit. If you don't know the power of Christ, it's time to do so, and if you do, maybe it's time to remind you of how vital He is to what you do.

How do we access God's power?

Let's go back to basics: the New Testament is very clear that the Holy Spirit inhabits every believer in Jesus, and gives us the power to do what we cannot naturally do. As Paul reminds us:

> *'You, however, are not in the realm of the flesh but are in*
> *the realm of the Spirit, if indeed the Spirit of God lives*
> *in you. And if anyone does not have the Spirit of*
> *Christ, they do not belong to Christ.'* (Rom. 8:9)

But our problem is that we can be believers (with the Holy Spirit within), but be practically powerless. It's like the batteries are in, but the electrodes in the wrong place.

The power issue is contentious. Churches have divided because members believed different things about God and what should be expected. We could fill this book reviewing various perspectives, but often the problem comes down to language and expectation. Sometimes both sides mean the same thing, but use different contemporary words to describe their life in God. Without going into a lengthy section on my doctrine of the Holy Spirit, here are a few salient points.

First, Jesus is filled with the Spirit at His baptism:

> *'As soon as Jesus was baptised, he went up out of the water.*
> *At that moment heaven was opened, and he saw the Spirit*
> *of God descending like a dove and alighting on him. And*
> *a voice from heaven said, "This is my Son, whom I love;*
> *with him I am well pleased."'* (Matt. 3:16–17)

It was necessary for Jesus, as fully man (and fully God), to know the empowering of the Holy Spirit.

In Acts 10, a sermon by the apostle Peter includes a reminder of how Jesus depended on the Holy Spirit:

'You know the message God sent to the people of Israel,
announcing the good news of peace through Jesus Christ,
who is Lord of all. You know what has happened
throughout the province of Judea, beginning in Galilee
after the baptism that John preached – how God
anointed Jesus of Nazareth with the Holy Spirit and power,
and how he went around doing good and healing all who
were under the power of the devil, because God was with
him.' (Acts 10:36–38, emphasis added)

We may not be able to get our heads around how Jesus is fully God and dependent on the Holy Spirit, but it's clearly something the New Testament affirms.

If you watch a man riding a motorbike fast, he will be little inspiration to you on your pushbike. Of course he's going fast – his bike has an engine. I had assumed that Jesus was a miracle-worker because He was God. Of course He's doing miracles – He's God! But that's not what the Bible says. Could it be that God was making sure that we couldn't just discard the example of Jesus as being irrelevant to us? Could it be that God wanted us to know that Jesus was also human like us, and just as He was able to perform miracles, so can we?

Jesus Himself anticipates the coming of the Spirit to the Church at Pentecost (after His ascension) when He says to His disciples:

'If you then, though you are evil, know how to give good
gifts to your children, how much more will your Father
in heaven give the Holy Spirit to those who ask him!'
(Luke 11:13)

Later, Paul would say to the churches in Galatia:

'After beginning by means of the Spirit, are you now
trying to finish by means of the flesh? Have you

experienced so much in vain – if it really was in
vain? So again I ask, does God give you his Spirit and
work miracles among you by the works of the law, or by
your believing what you heard?' (Gal. 3:3–5)

Open to the Spirit?

For a large part of my pastoral ministry I might have been like the
Galatians in that passage. I claimed to be open to the charismatic
movement, but in reality, I wasn't at all. I quite liked the odd story of
God at work, but in truth I was a long, long way from true openness.
At the time I was working in the offices at Premier Christian Radio as
a deputy editor of *Christianity* magazine. Gerald Coates, founder of
Pioneer, would occasionally pop in to do some recording and have a
word with my boss, John Buckeridge, who attended a Pioneer church,
and I would hear their conversation.

I had read articles about Gerald from evangelicals who claimed
that his theology was all over the place, and he wasn't to be trusted.
But there he was in the studio, larger than life, sharing stories from
his walk with God (of which I was envious). I have since shared with
him that he has unwittingly been a major part of my personal journey
in coming to realise the power of God available to us.

Some stories go viral, and it's easy to see why one from California
has been heard all around the world. One evening in 2004, Chad
Dedmon, on the staff at Bethel Church, went to buy doughnuts at
10pm. He went to his local Walmart and came across a cashier with a
hearing aid. His church encouraged people to look for opportunities
for God to move supernaturally, and so it was fairly natural for him to
ask if he could pray for her. She agreed, but clearly expected that he
would pray at home – and was somewhat surprised when he explained
that the healer was Jesus, and that he would pray for her right then
and there! The cashier was totally deaf in one ear and partially in the
other, and so having prayed, Chad needed to check her hearing by

speaking to her from various distances. It soon became evident that she had been completely healed in both ears, and to the delight of the onlookers and the other cashiers, she burst into tears of joy.

Chad sensed that there was still plenty of opportunity for God to move – so he asked to use the store's intercom. As he did so, God gave him words of knowledge for other shoppers – including someone needing a new hip, and someone else with carpal tunnel syndrome. He asked the cashier to tell her story over the intercom, and concluded her story by yelling: 'Attention all shoppers, God is in the building and is healing people in lane ten!'

Before long, people were looking down the aisles to see what was happening and (by Chad's estimation) 15–20 people gathered. This included a young woman in a motorised cart due for a hip replacement, who after prayer was able to move her legs without pain and then stand up. She shouted, 'Jesus just healed me!' several times before the small, bewildered crowd. A guy then pushed to the front and asked Chad if he thought God could heal his wrist. He was a concert pianist who'd had painful wrists for two years, and had said that as he'd entered the supermarket, he'd thought, 'Wouldn't it be great if the pain left tonight!' He too was miraculously and instantaneously healed. Realising that he then had quite a crowd, Chad shared the good news of Jesus, explaining what had happened, inviting any who wanted to know Jesus for themselves to raise their hands. A number of people did!

This story really challenged me and got me thinking about my own experiences. I've done a bit of open-air evangelism in my time. In Bournemouth, we had the opportunity to use the bandstand on a Sunday and would lead a few hymns, and myself and others would share a short message in between the singing. It was low key and pretty inoffensive. We had even tried a few things in the street, which attracted very few people. Chad's kind of story was on a different level.

I share it with you to illustrate the kind of things that I was aware God was doing. These stories puncture my scepticism and remind me that our God is an awesome God. There is a supernatural power that God intends us to have if we are to do His work and lead others.

How you know and sense the Holy Spirit may be different from other believers, and may vary from day to day. I have heard talks from those who regularly see healings who say they 'feel' nothing at all when they pray and see healing. So let's be wary of making too many assumptions about what the Holy Spirit may or may not do.

The presence of the Spirit

The Spirit's work is primarily seen in changing us so that we exhibit what Paul calls the fruit of the Spirit – love, joy, peace, forbearance, kindness, goodness, faithfulness, gentleness and self-control – the kind of things that make you a nice person to be around. It's here I believe we come to the biggest stumbling block to receiving the energy we need. The New Testament urges us to 'be filled with the Spirit' (Eph. 5:18), but also talks of our ongoing relationship *with* the Holy Spirit. We can grieve Him (Eph. 4:30) and quench Him (1 Thess. 5:19). In Ephesians 4, Paul goes on to explore the way in which our behaviour grieves the Spirit in the next verses:

> 'Get rid of all bitterness, rage and anger, brawling and
> slander, along with every form of malice. Be kind and
> compassionate to one another, forgiving each other,
> just as in Christ God forgave you.' (Eph. 4:31–32)

In other words, you can receive His energy, but your habits with your co-workers can lead the Holy Spirit to jump ship (so to speak) before you get to morning coffee! (The Holy Spirit will not actually leave, but you won't know His presence.) We all have the potential to know the Holy Spirit's empowering ministry if we are believers in Jesus and seek to follow Him. This is of course true irrespective of the denomination or church stream you are part of. But His presence may not be especially evident if we grieve Him. It will seem as if He has left us. Our sin, though wonderfully forgiven in Christ, will impair His work in our lives. There is no 'sin-o-meter' that we can consult to see how a particular sin or behaviour pattern affects the flow of the Spirit, but it is clear that sin functions like boulders within our lives, affecting the potentially powerful flow of the Spirit.

For some believers, the grieving of the Spirit is so pronounced that they know little of His empowering at all. This may be partly due to poor Bible teaching, lack of accountable relationships, or poor patterns of behaviour, all of which contribute to sinful patterns. To outsiders, it is barely evident that the person walks with Jesus at all. (I believe this is at the heart of why so many fail to walk the road less travelled.)

We can also quench the Spirit. The context is in failing to hear what He says through prophecy, but there is a wider sense of stifling what He seeks to do in our lives and that of the Church. How amazing that you and I can stifle God! Our understanding of the Holy Spirit's ministry links naturally to our level of expectation. When I claimed to be 'open to the charismatic movement', I actually had very little expectation in practice. It is therefore rather embarrassing to relate my first 'God used me in healing' story...

We were at Premier Radio studios for the weekly staff prayers for the editorial team, and my boss asked for prayers for his foot, which was giving him a lot of pain. We prayed for the other various requests, but since no one had yet prayed for John's foot, I offered a prayer. No one was more surprised than me when John said: 'My foot is getting hot. In my experience this is a sign that God is at work, please keep praying!'

Oh boy! I thought you prayed for stuff and maybe, just maybe, something might happen one day. But God was answering my prayer as I was praying! It led to considerable improvement in pain levels, though John did later need a visit to the doctor to get further help.

But the point is, expectation rises when God works. As we survey the Christian Church in the UK, we find that the churches that look to God to empower their people, pray for the filling of the Holy Spirit and pray for healing, see more than those that don't. Expectations and faith levels play a definite part.

If, in your leadership, you depend upon your own competence and hard work and effectively exclude God from what you lead, then you will know less of His help than if you are daily dependent and expectant. God is quite happy to take a back seat, though He is always keen and willing to be involved. Sometimes it really is as simple as 'you have not because you ask not'. And at one level, it can be very humbling to trust the Spirit. I can spend 20 hours crafting a message for a congregation. But uttering the words, 'come Holy Spirit' at the end, and waiting expectantly for Him to turn up, would produce massively more fruit!

As I have hinted already, my leadership has often had high doses of will power and not a lot of 'God power'. It seems I am not alone. Over ten years ago, one of my guests, Marcus Honeysett, formed a ministry called Living Leadership because he and others had noted that many ministers (especially men in their forties) had suffered burnout. Unable to continue in pastoral ministry they would move into other roles, perhaps in a charity, or back into the business world. In the purposes of God, neither should be regarded as second-class – but the feeling was that exhaustion and weariness of spirit were not ideal reasons for moving on, and it would be preferable if those in pastoral ministry continued to be refreshed by God and eager for the challenges He had for them within the local church. Marcus' assessment was that a large part of the problem was that many ministers hadn't learned to receive energy for the journey. They became dry, and they and their congregations suffered.

If you are serious about this journey, you will need to ask God to empower you. This is why He made you. It is time for you to join those whose leadership is marked by God, and He knows exactly how, when and what He needs to do within you. You may need some time away seeking Him. You may want to pray with a friend who understands these things. But whatever you do, *ask*. Christian leadership is leading in the ways of Christ, by the power of the Spirit. It's time to know His power.

....

Questions to consider

- How easy did you find this chapter? Talk to God about how you found it.
- When have you sensed God's power?
- When have you seen God's power? (Remember our senses can be unreliable.)

5. Walking with fellow travellers

'One of those days Jesus went out to a mountainside to pray, and spent the night praying to God. When morning came, he called his disciples to him and chose twelve of them, whom he also designated apostles: Simon (whom he named Peter), his brother Andrew, James, John, Philip, Bartholomew, Matthew, Thomas, James son of Alphaeus, Simon who was called the Zealot, Judas son of James, and Judas Iscariot, who became a traitor.'

(Luke 6:12–16)

It was an idyllic setting. The seawater was gently lapping against the rocks close to the beach, and there was a pleasant coolness to the evening, contrasting the scorching heat we had endured during the day. I was the speaker on my first Oak Hall Holiday in Varkiza, Greece, at the beginning of a month I would spend there – the first two weeks as a speaker, the next two as a leader. (Oak Hall Holidays is a Christian holiday company, running optional worship and teaching sessions each evening.) It was 1988, and preparing to start as a staff worker with UCCF that autumn, I had come prepared to deliver talks from the book of James. We had our first session with the thirty or so people who were on the holiday, and afterwards I was chatting with the leader of the trip, a guy called Phil Carter. He asked me how I thought the time had gone.

'Pretty well,' I said. I had spoken on James before, and the first session was setting the scene for the book and looking at part of the first chapter.

Phil smiled. 'Look, the content is great. Trouble is, no one wants to hear it! It was all true, but didn't connect with where they are in life.'

It wasn't exactly what I had wanted to hear. But Phil seemed like a nice guy, and was clearly trying to help me. *He must care,* I thought. So rather than react defensively, I simply asked: 'So, what do you suggest?' I was guessing, correctly, that he might have some insights.

'Look, don't get me wrong. Your content really is great. My problem is that I can connect with people, but then don't have anything to tell them. You have stuff to tell, but people will be lost before you get to it. So maybe we could work together on your introductions, so you connect better, and then they will want to hear what you have to say – and God will work.'

So that's what we did. We would find a time during the day for me to precis what I was going to say. Phil would then make suggestions on how to better connect with the underlying feelings of those attending, and in the evening I would give a revamped talk. And I have to agree – it went much, much better. Indeed, such was the bond that Phil and

I built that he offered me a place in his bachelor pad in Reading as a base for my work with UCCF – a place that was my home until his marriage three years into my four-year stint with the ministry. Along with my brother, he would be best man at my own wedding.

We were – quite literally – fellow travellers, and formed something of a team for that brief but significant fortnight. There's absolutely no doubt that walking the leadership road less travelled is rarely walked alone. You need fellow travellers.

Now, there's a good chance you may need convincing that this is the case. Many leaders are, by nature, solo types. It kind of goes with the territory. The things that make someone stand out from the crowd can also be things that are isolating. And you may well be reading this as someone who, frankly, likes their own company.

If you have come across the Myers–Briggs Type Indicator, you will know that a good number – roughly 50% in fact – are on the introvert end of the scale.[1] It is a misnomer to say that 'introvert' is synonymous with 'loner'. In fact, what the Myers–Briggs indicator is saying is that some derive energy from their inner world, rather than the external one. An introvert loves parties if they can find a few people with whom they can have in-depth chats and nurture their inner world. But it would be true that introverts *think* they can survive on their own, because they can nurture their inner world via books and podcasts. It would also be true that they can find extraverts exhausting. Why would one want to team up with others who might disrupt them from their God-given goals? (I personally sit more towards the introvert end of the spectrum than the extravert end.)

Indeed, in some church leadership circles, those scoring more highly on introversion form the majority. The role of a vicar is classically solo, and includes long periods of time spent alone (in study, in prayer, in reflection). One survey of Anglican ordinands found that most were introverts.[2]

Of course, both extraverts and introverts read, but since introversion and reading are good friends, there will be a high chance that many readers of this book will be in the introvert camp. If that's you, you may need convincing that teaming up really is good news. And even if you are firmly in the extravert camp, don't know what you would be, or are frankly sceptical about the whole scene, it's still good to remember why we need fellow travellers!

By 'fellow travellers' I don't necessarily mean fellow colleagues. You may well be leading in a non-believing environment. Whether you work with fellow Christians or not, I'm talking about people who are seeking to lead in the way of Christ in the power of the Spirit, and who understand the challenges you face and can pray for you and cheer you on.

It's how God arranged it

God clearly arranged for life to be lived in community, starting with the family unit. We know from Genesis that 'It is not good for man to be alone' (Gen. 2:18). For many people, marriage is their main way of meeting the loneliness need. Indeed, at the very beginning, God mandates that man and woman are co-rulers. The ruling function is given to both. Of course, Jesus and Paul were both unmarried – so it's clear that stunning ministry is possible without a partner! But singles still need teams, as we will see later.

If you are married, ideally your partner will understand, value and support what you are trying to do. The degree to which this is possible of course varies, and this is not intended to be guilt-inducing if you and your spouse have different working worlds and no real partnership with each other in those roles (providing that other areas of marriage are flourishing). Your leadership of the home together is a key place in which the road is walked. The family has at times been idolatrous within some Christian communities, when people have forgotten that Jesus has first priority, but you don't have to worship the family to realise that your responsibility for providing God-like care and nurture is vital.

The child you bring up will one day be introduced to the love of God. How great if they know what that is because they already received it from you!

As the father of two adopted sons, I have been given fresh insights into how God adopts us unconditionally. I want to care for them, coach and support them so that they get a taste of how God feels about them, and how He longs for them to reach their potential. If you are a parent, I'm sure you feel the same. But married or not, and whether your spouse understands or not, if you are walking in the way of Christ by the power of the Spirit, you need someone to pray with you, commiserate when you are misunderstood, and assure you that walking the way of the Master – though counter-cultural – is the right thing to do.

The dream team

Just as there was a point when Israel wanted a king like the other nations, many churches have opted for a key person as their leader. And let's face it – practicalities are often a factor. You may have just enough money for one salary, or the denomination is only funding one person. That's understood. But if you take a look at the New Testament, you don't find that churches are led by just one person. The leadership is always corporate.

Paul refers to the 'elders' (plural) in Acts 20:28, and 'elders' (plural) in his letters (Titus 1:5; 1 Tim. 3:8–13). When the apostle Peter addresses his fellow believers in his epistles, he refers to himself as a 'fellow elder' and encourages them to recognise that God is the chief shepherd to whom they are all accountable. It is sometimes assumed that Timothy and Titus are the exception, since their's are 'pastoral epistles' and the assumption is made that each operated solo. But there is no such designation in the text. Timothy and Titus were apostolic emissaries, who were sent to Ephesus and Crete (respectively) for temporary duties, to assist in particular matters with respect to the Church. Indeed, in the case of Titus, he was specifically instructed to put elders (plural) in place.

John Stott, who was himself a rector at All Souls Langham Place, London, said this:

> 'So Godly leaders serve, indeed "serve not their own interests but rather the interests of others" (Phil. 2:4). This simple principle should deliver the leader from excessive individualism, extreme isolation, and self-centered empire-building. For those who serve others serve best in a team.'[3]

In practice, we may find that an individual may function as the *primus inter pares* (the first among equals), and often the supported worker or senior person in a church team will have a skippering function. Someone can still take a 'lead', and needs to be free to do so; corporate leadership does not always mean leadership by consensus, as if every single leader has to rubber-stamp every decision. Therein lies chaos and inertia and we are wise to have systems that have appropriate checks and balances.

If you lead in a church setting, ideally the whole church is on board with walking the leadership road less travelled. I remember reading of one church in Colorado who would ask every prospective church member: 'What is your ministry?'[4] The assumption was that the Holy Spirit dwelt in them and was looking to utilise them for His kingdom. If it didn't cost inordinate amounts of money or fellow members, the response from the leadership would be to ask: 'So how can we best equip you for that ministry?' They had understood that the New Testament sees us all as priests. A new member is not merely a source of income for the church leaders' plans and projects, or an extra person to utilise in the church projects. They have a ministry. How can it be fulfilled?

Hence the New Testament model is that every believer looks

to serve the purposes of Christ within the body of Christ. Those designated leaders (whatever they are called) lead mindful that the Spirit of Christ is with each member, looking to equip every believer to serve wherever they are placed – in families, in the workplace, in education, in circles of influence with friends and those in the community. They don't cajole anyone to their agenda, except where they believe God is leading – and even then gently and graciously, with awareness that they may be wrong.

Frank Viola writes:

> 'When we read words like "pastor", "overseer", and "elder", we immediately think in terms of governmental offices like "president", "senator", and "chairman". So we regard elders, pastors, and overseers as sociological constructs (offices). We view them as vacant slots that possess a reality independent of the persons who populate them. We then ascribe mere men with unquestioned authority simply because they "hold office"... The basic tasks of biblical leadership are facilitation, nurture, guidance, and service. To the degree that a member is modeling the will of God in one of those areas, to that degree he or she is leading. It's no wonder that Paul never chose to use any of the forty-plus common Greek words for "office" and "authority" when discussing leaders. Again, Paul's favorite word for describing leadership is the opposite of what natural minds would suspect. It's diakonos, which means a "servant"—a person very low on the social totem pole in the 1st Century.'[5]

You may be in a leadership role where position and authority structure is part of the organisation, and you can't stride into work announcing a flat structure overnight. But you might find it helpful to consider John Maxwell's 'levels of leadership' approach. In his book *Developing the Leader Within You*,[6] he outlines his five levels of leadership. The very first level of leadership is when you lead by 'position'. People have to follow you because you have the position above them, and the organisation insists that this is what you have to do. There might be penalties if you don't (the kind of leadership exercised by the Romans). Some only ever see their leadership in terms of position, but Maxwell would say that this is only the first level of leadership.

The second level is 'permission', whereby people follow because they want to. The level of relationship is such that people connect with the leader and follow them, because of who they are and not just their position in the organisation.

The third level, 'production', reflects the way in which leaders are followed because of what they do for the team or organisation. Leaders at this level are seen as achievers, and are followed for their good accomplishments on behalf of the whole group.

The fourth level is 'people development'. Here the leader is not just productive, but helps others develop their leadership; they raise the collective capacity to lead further.

Maxwell finally suggests a fifth level, which just 1% of people accomplish: 'pinnacle'. This refers to those who develop level-four leaders, and are followed because of who they are and what they represent.

So even if you are in a leadership role with clear hierarchy, your leadership road less travelled is to serve those under you, that they may be the best they can be, maybe even to that pinnacle level described by Maxwell.

Look at the ministry of Jesus. He had a band of 12 men, and was especially close to three of them – Peter, James and John – with John seemingly the closest to Him. Jesus sent groups of His followers two by two to join in His work of preaching the kingdom, healing the sick and casting out demons.

Look at how Paul operated. He mostly travelled with others:

Barnabas, Silas, Luke. He had Timothy and Titus as his apostolic emissaries. Priscilla and Aquila, Epaphras, Epaphroditus, Philemon and a host of others were mentioned as part of his team, or as those who worked in the churches he planted. Of course there were times when Paul operated solo (see Acts 17:16), but these were rare.

How God makes Himself known

When I began as a staff worker with UCCF we had a visit from the greatly respected Nigel Lee, who had served with OM (Operation Mobilisation) and was an itinerant Bible teacher (he would later serve as Head of Student Ministries with UCCF before his death from cancer aged just 51). I recall his message about the way in which the spiritual life of a CU's leadership team is crucial to the life of the entire CU, not just in what it does, but in terms of who they are as a group. He explained that their mutual love and commitment to one another becomes the seedbed for other godly connections that will ripple from that core. If the leaders don't get on, it will be hard for the CU to flourish.

This is how the life of God is manifest as we serve, love, encourage, rebuke and nurture *one another*. In the New Testament epistles there are no less than 44 *one anothers*. Paul assumes and encourages a 'body' life – not a life dictated by leaders, but one where the whole body nurtures one another according to their gifting, maturity and season of life. That is how you will find great joy in your fellow travellers.

Fellow travellers pick you up when you are down, and share stories that link with you. I have been blessed by those who have stood by me in an academic disaster, when the dream of pastoral ministry fell apart and when I made the transition to journalism for a time. Phil, Mark, Steve, Paul, Terry, Hugo – thank you. Do you have a similar list? And this is not to mention the countless times my wife and immediate family have borne with me and my ups and downs, pulled me back to my feet and watched me put one foot in front of the other until I could walk the journey again.

Leadership will have its tough times – times that don't make sense. There will be times when others let us down (and times when we let ourselves down and are feeling bad because it was our fault and no one else's), and we will need our friends to draw alongside us and suggest a diversion, or invite us for a coffee and a chat, and articulate what we were vaguely thinking but couldn't find words for.

I said earlier that those who wish to walk the leadership road less travelled rarely walk alone. The word 'rarely' was deliberate. There will be times when Christian leaders are alone in their leading. Perhaps you are the only director of the company who is a Christian. Perhaps you are on a leadership team in a charity that thinks differently to you about how to serve Jesus. Perhaps you have started as a minister in a church that doesn't yet value what you value. For you, I would say that it's important for you to find fellow travellers outside your setting with whom you can enjoy fellowship on a semi-regular basis. The culture in which you operate will swallow you up if you don't have a dedicated and buoyant personal life with God, and people around you who get what you are trying to do and will support you.

Finding fellow travellers

Finding fellow travellers isn't always easy. If you are comfortable on your own, you may not experience pain or isolation enough to feel especially motivated. But you will be glad you did.

Get out more

Join networks in your field, attend conferences, seminars, ministers' fraternities, etc. Even if your interest is marginal, make the effort to attend. Look to see if there is a Christian fellowship in your company, or field of work. Don't attend acting like a single person desperate for a partner, but gently ask God to lead you to connect with people.

Invite yourself for coffee

Some of my fellow travellers have become so because I asked if I could meet with them. You don't have to go with any agenda, and you may not 'click' – but at the very least you will have made an acquaintance, and at the best a friend.

Involve others in what you are doing

I know people in the church world who won't do ministry if they can't take a younger person with them. My friend Steve Brady (now Principal of Moorlands College) took me on preaching trips way before I ever worked in a church. It whetted my appetite to get involved myself, and it was always great fun. But the point is that some of these will, in time, become fellow travellers with you.

Social media

OK, you can't exactly advertise your need for a fellow traveller on Twitter. But as you read various online posts, blogs and tweets, you can get an idea of where people are coming from. It may be a 'can we chat on the phone or email?' kind of conversation, or a chance to meet in person. Hosting a radio show gives me a great excuse to connect with others, and I have made a number of friends this way. But you can too (with or without a radio station).

Developing future travellers

If you are becoming convinced that leading in the way of Christ in the power of the Spirit is 'the' way to lead, then you will be wanting to inspire others to take this route too. How great would it be if your church was multiplying the capacity of its members to be an influence where God has placed them, by encouraging a Christ-centred, Spirit-inspired outlook? Who can you encourage to start the journey?

People matter

When I was researching what Christians in leadership look for in terms of support, I wrote to around a hundred Christian leaders who had been my guests on *The Leadership File*. John Sutherland[7] replied. He served as a commander in the police force and has been a friend for several decades, since his days as a student at Reading University. In his reply to me, he talked about his approach to leadership by adjusting the oft-quoted slogan from Bill Clinton's 1992 presidential campaign: 'It's the economy, stupid.' In his email to me, John said: 'It's about people, stupid.' His leadership maxim is to make sure he focuses on people. As a leader, how can he lead those 'under him' to do their jobs better?

As a leader you will have many tasks to accomplish and will probably measure your success against them, but when you look back, it won't be the to-do lists ticked and the metrics measured that will fill your memories. It will be the people you walked with.

Who journeys with you?

....

Questions to consider
- Who could you spend time with that might help you to think like Jesus?
- Is there someone you know you could approach?
- Who might advise you on people that you could meet with?
- Are there key thinkers you might never meet, but can read or listen to?

6. Finding direction

*'And Jesus came and said to them,
"All authority in heaven and on earth has
been given to me. Go therefore and make
disciples of all nations, baptising them
in the name of the Father and of the Son
and of the Holy Spirit, teaching them to
observe all that I have commanded you.
And surely, I am with you always, to the
end of the age."'* (Matt. 28:18–20)

My wife is a schoolteacher, and she's especially good at teaching maths. Why? Is she a good mathematician? Far from it – she achieved her maths O-level (GCSE) on her third attempt, after plenty of extra tutoring. She knew she needed it because, without it, she couldn't enter her dream profession. She's a good teacher because she found maths challenging herself, and understands why children may find it tough too. She knows the path well, and she has stayed focused.

As I mentioned in the introduction, 'finding direction' has often been a challenge for me. Look at someone's bookshelf and it will tell you what they are interested in or struggling with. My own bookshelf, heaving with 'guidance' titles, speaks for itself. I have books from a variety of perspectives – from the school of 'God speaks through His Word and nowhere else' to the school of 'conversational prayer', where God seems to be chatting ceaselessly about all manner of things. And I have been convinced of different views at various points in my journey – changing so often at times that I've thought it was tough for even God to keep up. The bedrock has been, 'So, what does Scripture teach?', and my views have changed according to careful exposition from teachers and writers who, at least for a moment, won me over.

The topic of guidance and direction is of course central to a book subtitled 'Leading as God intended you to' – and I've found that, for so many Christian leaders, there is little or no focus to their activities. So what am I discovering that may be helpful to you? Well, to start with, for a time I believed that God had a will that I needed to discover in order to find my destiny and live fruitfully for Him. Like many people who look for guidance in the world, it became a highly subjective and ultimately impoverishing approach. Circumstances would come into play – was this an open door, or a diversion from God's pathway? Were my feelings about a decision relevant, or was I to make a strictly rational decision? I found that I was uncertain too often, and complaining at God for not making it clear – then backtracking and concluding that it must be me being a dunderhead.

Then I had my 'It's all in the Bible' phase, encouraged by *Decision Making and the Will of God* by Garry Friesen and J. Robin Maxson.[1] It looks at the three 'wills' of God we might concern ourselves with: His sovereign will (which will happen regardless), His moral will (as revealed in Scripture), and an individual will (regarding the details of our individual lives). The book argues that God's sovereign will is something we accept rather than seek. It's going to happen. We are responsible for following the moral will as revealed in Scripture: the commands, properly understood, become our guide, with God helping us.

But Friesen and Maxson believe there is no 'individual will' of God for each and every person, and so we have liberty and freedom thereafter to choose as we see fit. God is not going to guide us in those details, so we relax and exercise our responsible judgment. This will include such humdingers as who we marry, what job we do, where we live, where we worship and – in the topic of this book – what and who we lead, and whether we lead. Friesen believes, therefore, that our decisions in this regard fall not into the 'right or wrong' category, but the 'wise or foolish'. For example, you are free to marry anyone who is a believer (according to the moral will where we are commanded to marry in the Lord), but it would foolish to choose someone to whom you are attracted but with whom you have little emotional connection and shared interests. You are free to choose any job, providing it is legitimate, but you are foolish to choose one that would be damaging to your health and time spent with family.

So I went along with that way of thinking for a while. It freed me up considerably, and I was even 'preaching' to friends who were muddled by trying the tightrope approach. And I still think it has value. But I was entering my 'more obviously open to the charismatic' phase, and I was becoming more aware that God speaks into the hearts and minds of His people, so that we sense what is the correct way.

My journey into journalism began after I'd spent some time trying to get back into pastoral ministry. My time on a 'breather' in leafy Surrey was lasting rather longer than expected, and all my looking into working with various churches hadn't led to any work. Maybe God hadn't equipped me to be a pastor after all…?

I had begun working on a writing project with HarperCollins and decided that, since I enjoyed writing, maybe I should follow a childhood dream of becoming a journalist (I wanted to feel a little more connected to the 'real world' too). So I completed a fast-track NVQ qualification in journalism, and was looking for work. I had two interviews: one with *Power* magazine (a trade magazine serving the energy industry), which was located just a couple of miles away and ticked the 'connection with the real world' box. The other was with *Christianity* magazine, based in Premier Christian Radio (not far from Victoria station). Both interviews went well. The salaries offered were roughly the same when the cost of commuting was factored in. Both companies offered me a job, and I had a weekend to decide.

Now remember I was armed with this new belief that God would let me know what He wanted. After all, this was a major decision that would affect a good chunk of each week and my first full-time role after pastoral ministry. Did God want me to work for *Power* magazine and connect back with colleagues and customers outside the Church, or for *Christianity* magazine, which was slap bang in the middle of the Christian bubble – indeed, helping to perpetuate it?

I prayed. Nothing. I asked God to speak any way He chose: dreams, impressions, surprise phone calls, emails. On the Sunday, with time running out, I was looking for anything in the hymns or sermons that might fit! Advice from friends? A few said to go for *Christianity*, but I suspect that's because they knew more about that than energy. It came to Monday morning and I still had no idea what God 'wanted'. He had said precisely nothing. Or had He?

Looking back, I believe He did speak. He was saying, 'Andy – you decide. I am with you in either decision. You have your heart on pleasing me. I am happy with whatever you do.'

In the absence of any clarity, I had to decide. I knew about Christianity so figured I could do a job for the magazine, based on what I knew. I also figured I would enjoy writing *about* Christianity. (I had no idea whether I would have enjoyed writing about energy quite so much, and the shorter commute didn't counteract that uncertainty.) I chose *Christianity*.

I have now entered a phase of understanding guidance that I have been in for some time, not least because I now run a course on it. I believe God has plans and purposes and will accomplish all that He intends. But His dealings with us as His people in Scripture suggest a relational component that is stronger than I ever thought possible. I believe that we have far more choices within certain parameters than I previously imagined. He longs to take us deeper into His love and ways, and is much smarter and more flexible and more tailor-made in His dealings with us than I previously thought. He is the very best Dad, who guides His children. At times there are ways He knows are best and He lets us know. But our wills are precious things, and He is keen that we choose for Him and grow in our love, even as we live life together.

So here are my top tips for staying on track.

1. Follow Jesus as best you can

That's right – we're back to this theme again! But at the heart of all guidance is this willingness to obey all that Jesus says to you. (This includes Friesen's moral will, but also anything else that you test and believe may be from Him.) Following Jesus means that some element of your 'mission' is already determined: you are to make disciples. Your role in that may be different to mine, but it needs to be at the top of the agenda, whatever or whoever you lead. This leads to you changing over time, developing a heart for the things that God cares about, and being more open to the kinds of things that concern Him. He cares deeply about your maturity and character.

2. Know yourself

I believe we are wise to know as much as we can about ourselves as we make guidance decisions. There are online tools that are a great help. I have used Myers–Briggs Type Indicator, Strengthfinder, DISC and the thematic apperceptive test run by McClelland.

These kinds of personality testing are designed to give you an outline of your typical traits. Is this kind of 'analysis' vital? No. But knowing yourself involves knowing how you typically feel about decisions and advisors, about hunches and feelings, and sensing certainty. They will be unique to you, and testable over time. (And not only that, it's really affirming.)

3. Know your gifts and talents

This is all part of knowing yourself, but is more specific. If you have gifts and talents (and we all do!), it makes sense to use them for the benefit of others. Many churches run gift discovery courses (I run one at CWR, if you are not sure). The principle of 'do what you are good at' is not rocket science. Remember, God has made you in His image to rule. You will have a preference for certain aspects of this ruling. That will be a clue to how your gifts and talents may be deployed.

4. Know your heart

We are encouraged to seek gifts – and how you would like to be empowered and used is also part of the equation. God may use your broken heart or your sense of pain and sadness at something to propel you into something even greater for His purposes.

Keeping focus

My belief is that finding focus and keeping focus are two different things, and the chances are that finding your focus is only part of the problem. Knowing what we might do, or could do, is only part of the challenge. Many leaders are in a job they can do, and enjoy doing… but are still enormously frustrated. There's another element to all this that's worth looking at. The leadership road less travelled is the one where leaders are able to stick to their task with enthusiasm.

Our present world offers limitless opportunities for distraction. Even as I type, I am mere moments away from accessing my football team's latest news and emails from friends. All I have to do is move the mouse. But these are really just 'level one' distractions. Most leaders have a bunch of what I call 'level two' distractions too. Name almost any leadership task and you have choices – and the fear of making the wrong choice – and so the need to research the options and consider the outcomes of others who have made that choice. It's exhausting. At times you need to pay due diligence, but you are wise to set limits.

Psychiatrist Peter Shallard, who calls himself 'the shrink for entrepreneurs', believes that this capacity to be distracted is a particularly western phenomenon, born out of the kind of sedentary lives we now live, and is largely industrialised. We are able to have our shopping delivered at the click of the mouse, rather than having to get our hands dirty with livestock or crops. We don't need a get-up-and-go side to life. From his work with start-up entrepreneurs, Shallard paints a picture of people thrilled to be getting the chance to develop their own businesses, but failing to be productive. Procrastination is a major disease. We are overwhelmed with options. We end up doing nothing.

The 'why' factor

Knowing *why* we do what we do is very powerful. Most people who are burned out are not overworked, but have lost their sense of purpose. Of paramount importance is to remind yourself why you became a leader in the first place. Plenty of people looked at the leadership option in life and said, 'No thanks, it's not for me.' But you didn't. You are a leader (or aspiring to be one and reading this book). Why? What was it that caused you to put your head above the parapet?

Why are you leading a church or charity? Why are you leading a home group? How come you decided to accept a role leading your department? Why did you and your spouse decide to have children?

I appreciate that you may have sensed a distinct experience of God that amounted to a call to service. But whether you sensed that or not, you hopefully also have a reason *why* you are leading.

In his book *Start with Why: How Great Leaders Inspire Everyone To Take Action*, Simon Sinek put it like this:

> '*It all starts with clarity. You have to know WHY you do WHAT you do. If people don't buy WHAT you do, they buy WHY you do it, so it follows that if you don't know WHY you do WHAT you do, how will anyone else? If the leader of the organization can't clearly articulate WHY the organization exists in terms beyond its products or services, then how does he expect the employees to know WHY to come to work? If a politician can't articulate WHY she seeks public office beyond the standard "to serve the people" (the minimum rational standard for all politicians), then how will the voters know whom to follow?*'[2]

Sinek's whole book unwraps the importance of discovering (or rediscovering) your 'why', and ruthlessly applying it to your life. It is not uncommon for leaders to lose that sense of why they became a leader in the first place, especially if they have been leading for a while. If that has happened to you, rediscovering your 'why' is crucial to having a sense of momentum and energy in your life and leading.

Working out the 'why'

There's a whole host of reasons why you may be leading, and of course, some are more altruistic than others. Why you lead could include:

'I wanted to boss others around.'

'I wanted people to listen to me.'

'Because I am good at it!'

'It's what I always wanted to do.'

'I believed in the cause and so started it.'

'I wanted a job with more pay than I was getting.'

'I thought I would be good at it – turns out I'm not, but I can't move.'

'If I wasn't leading it, I would have to put up with someone else!'

'No one else will do it and I don't want it to fold.'

'I am going through the motions because fellow leaders won't back what I really want to do.'

Sinek suggests we will struggle to stay focused in our leadership without a compelling 'why' and, most importantly, we will struggle to inspire those we lead if we aren't sure why we are doing so. In many cases, inspiration may not matter. If those who follow us are paid to do so, then we will have processes to ensure they follow the policy of the company or charity. But true leadership helps people to go the extra mile, and join willingly in the work.

I have interviewed people with a crystal-clear 'why', who come alive when they talk about what they lead. I think in particular of Pete Carter leading Eastgate Church in Gravesend, convinced that God has called him to lead a church that sees a revival culture develop. I think of Buddy Reeve, who heads up a ministry to the old people's homes in Eastbourne, keen that the elderly might have the opportunity to be reminded of (or hear for the first time) the gospel, and enjoy hymns they know and love. That's the kind of leadership that spurs people to choose willingly to give themselves for the cause. If you are a church leader, you have volunteers who serve Christ with you, but will walk away if they sense that what you are doing together is not worthy of their best efforts. Your 'why' can be their 'why' if you know what it is and inspire them to follow you.

So often the 'why' is what leads you to become a leader in the first place. Anne-Marie Wilson was a medical relief nurse in Sudan who was so upset by the plight of young African girls enduring female genital mutilation (FGM) that she founded the charity 28 Too Many in 2010 (the title reflects the number of countries where FGM is practised). She was not a 'leader' as such – she was a nurse – but became a leader to further the cause.

It may take you a while to figure out your 'why'. Some questions may help:

- Can you recall the first time you ever led something? What was your motivation then?
- What kind of outcomes would be pleasing to you in the areas you are leading? (Profits? Funds raised? Is it people? Fellow colleagues flourishing in their God-given gifts? People understanding truth? Coming to faith? Is it having a well-run organisation? Is it accomplishing more than you have ever done?)
- What kinds of activities do you enjoy?
- What activities can you lose yourself in?

You may need to spend time with Jesus reflecting on your journey and what brings you to this point in time. If you are honest and find that you had mixed motives, you may want to ask Jesus to help you see the opportunity through His eyes. Many start leading for selfish reasons, only to discover a greater sense of service as time goes by.

Someone else's 'why'

The 'why' issue is especially important if you are leading something that someone else started, or where the agenda is set by others. Grasping and approving that 'why' will be important; hopefully that happened when you were interviewed for the role. But it may be that the default 'why' is a bit different from the actual 'why'. The field I know best – the Church world – is replete with churches that have forgotten why they exist and why they were set up, and why they should exist according to the New Testament. They may have pleasant-sounding language in their mission statement, but you can tell the actual 'why' by looking at what they do. Good leadership helps people realise that the true 'why' is worthy of their best efforts, though it can take a long while to bring people back on track. But the most important thing is that you as leader are convinced that the 'why' is worth it, and don't lose your nerve as you enthuse others.

Figuring out the 'what'

If you know 'why' you are leading, you then need to look at the 'what': what do you need to do to accomplish the 'why'?

David Allen (author of *Getting Things Done*) and Stephen Covey (author of *Seven Habits of Highly Effective People*) are excellent at helping readers identify how they can make their 'why' work.

In his book, *The One Thing: The Surprisingly Simple Truth Behind Extraordinary Results*, Gary Keller takes time management a step further. He is critical of those who are driven by to-do lists, because he believes they create a temptation for us to be pressured to 'do' what's on the list without reviewing what it is we are doing. You could conceivably tick off your 20 to-dos, but either you'll miss doing the things that were truly important, or fail to proportion time in favour of what truly matters. He says: 'Go extreme. Once you've figured out what actually matters, keep asking what matters most until there is only one thing left. That core activity goes at the top of your success list.'[3]

This core activity will change over time. But if we know the one thing that we are focusing on, we can make sure that we take daily steps towards it. For Patrick Regan, it was stamping out knife crime.

He had been working as a youth worker when, in 1996, someone was stabbed in the playground of a school he visited. The head teacher asked Patrick to go in to help deal with behaviour issues and, in time, a charity now known as XLP (eXceL Project) was born. XLP works with young people in urban areas, helping to provide a better future for them. Patrick had focused on one thing.

Keller advises the following:

> 'Start each day by asking, "What's the ONE thing I can do today for [whatever you want] such that by doing it everything else will be easier or even unnecessary?" When you do this, your direction will become clear. Your work will be more productive and your personal life more rewarding.'[4]

A church leader who believes their 'one thing' is growing the church might want to prioritise training people to share their faith more adequately. A charity worker whose 'one thing' is raising funds may discover that their 'one thing' is getting some help on presenting the charity to outsiders.

Major General Tim Cross

It might seem a bit obvious for me to turn to the armed forces for examples of leaders that have found direction, but my interview with Major General Tim Cross painted a slightly different picture to what I had expected. It was a great joy to be able interview him – not least because at the time he was 'a hot news item' for his comments regarding the poverty of planning following the war in Iraq.

As the Senior Army Officer, Cross had cautioned Prime Minister Tony Blair and US Defense Secretary Donald Rumsfeld about entering into conflict with Saddam Hussein without having a plan for what would follow. He had questioned the naivety of an approach that assumed that the Iraqi people would welcome the allies with open arms and turn upon the Hussein regime. Giving evidence to the Iraq Inquiry, he had urged politicians to delay the invasion, and called the post-war planning 'woefully thin'.

Of course he was later proved right, and we discussed the leadership lessons during our radio interview. I asked him whether his faith had ever played a significant role in operations, presuming that perhaps as an army commander, there would be little room for such matters. His response was that the Balkan War left a potential humanitarian disaster. He had served in three tours of the Balkans, and it was the third that was especially significant, as he was responsible for co-ordinating multinational troops and civilian agencies in establishing refugee camps in the aftermath of the Kosovo War – which led to his appointment as a Commander of the Order of the British Empire (CBE) for his service. Although decorated for the action, this was not strictly army business. Cross said he doubted he would have engaged in the co-ordination work if his faith had not informed his concern for those struggling in the aftermath of the war. Here was a man who focused on his mission as a follower of Jesus, while engaging in an army-based mission.

Your schedule

Once you know your 'why' and your 'one thing', you need to make sure you stick to it. In January 2015, Bill Hybels (Senior Pastor of Willow Creek Community Church, Chicago) gave a talk to his congregation on what he termed 'the crazy power of the schedule'. Like Keller, he cautioned against the 'to-do list mentality', and urged the congregation to think in terms of who they wanted to become. He used the illustration of how, as a grandparent, he was desperate to make sure he got to know his grandsons – and so whenever he is home, he has an appointment with them every Saturday morning inked into his schedule. He says: 'If you want to be different in the future, work out what actions you need to take to get you there and put them in your diary.'

The advice is not especially new, but is seldom practised. If you think about who you want to become in the future, you have it within you to make a start. There will be material in this book that will help you to get going. Your planner/diary/calendar/schedule is a great place to kick off. Your calendar tells you who you are and your calendar never lies.

You are unlikely to change your focus unless you are convinced in your head and heart that this is the way ahead. Someone in love doesn't have to 'choose' to focus on a date with their beloved. If you are captivated by a sunset, you are not distracted by browsing on your smartphone.

But scheduling our priorities is just one half of the equation. Let's be open to the fact that God's timetable is often very different to ours. Within Jesus' overall purposes, there were plenty of mini-moments that seemed unpredictable. We find that things aren't quite as we expected; planned events are different from anticipated. A new element enters the equation and we have to adjust. It is foolish to just carry on regardless at such times. Going with what God seems to be doing and saying at any moment is a priority. And the skill of spotting when God is at work, redirecting you, overruling through circumstance, speaking into your heart and mind, is one that comes with time.

If Christian leaders have a bias, it is probably towards being planned and structured, rather than being open to the Spirit. The left-brain, type-A personality is keen to act powerfully to make a difference, creating the future they wish to live in. If you know that's you, why not give God room to speak? If you are more spontaneous by nature, remember that God can speak anytime – including the times when we have the diary and calendar out.

....

Questions to consider

- Why do you lead?
- What is your 'one thing'?
- Have a look at your diary presently. What does this say about your life and who you want to become? What needs to change?

7. Adopting the right mindset

'We demolish arguments and every pretension that sets itself up against the knowledge of God, and we take captive every thought to make it obedient to Christ.' (2 Cor. 10:5)

In the film *The Iron Lady* (2011), British Prime Minister Margaret Thatcher (played by Meryl Streep) is asked by her therapist how she is feeling. She gives a robust reply about the way in which her feelings are really of no consequence, but it is how she is thinking that should be of concern: 'Watch your thoughts, for they become words. Watch your words, for they become actions. Watch your actions, for they become habits. Watch your habits, for they become your character. And watch your character, for it becomes your destiny. What we think, we become. My father always said that. And I *think* I am fine.'[1]

Whether or not you are charmed by Thatcher's approach, her views of the importance of thinking are accurate. How you think is a pivotal part of your whole life. Your thoughts imprison or liberate you, encourage you or drag you down. It is thought that as many as 80% of the thoughts of the average person are negative, either towards themselves or others.

My hope and prayer is that some of God's thinking about leadership will change the way you think and act. But the effects of this will be very temporary unless you adopt a new mindset, which is nourished and fueled regularly by godly input. We do not operate in neutral territory. We are bombarded with daily messages about what to think and believe about our world. Some are relatively harmless and will have very little long-term effect, but over time, they will seep into our minds and hearts if we do not take action.

We have recently installed software on our boys' phones to protect them from unwanted internet material, reasoning that we wouldn't leave our front door wide open in a hostile neighbourhood. Likewise, we need to have equivalent means of shielding ourselves from alternative ways of leading others, which might sound enticing and successful but would lead us far from the way of Christ. We need to take care that unhealthy views of God don't colour our thinking. The Lutheran astronomer and theologian Johannes Kepler described science as 'thinking God's thoughts after Him'.[2] In a very real sense, this is what we seek to do as we look at the world before us and our roles as leaders within it. As believers in Jesus, we are learning how to see the world as He does. Any actions we take as leaders are to be based upon that central premise.

Dallas Willard gives this helpful definition of 'thinking':

> 'By "thoughts" we mean all of the ways in which we are conscious of things—and it includes our memories, perceptions and beliefs. Thoughts determine the orientation of everything we do and evoke the feelings that frame our world and motivate our actions. Interestingly, you can't evoke thoughts by feeling a certain way. However, we can evoke—and to some degree—control our feelings by directing our thoughts.'[3]

Thinking is such a vital part of leadership, and we need to find time for it. Successful CEO and company president, Dan Cathy, is reported to have said that thinking is so important to him that he devotes half a day a fortnight, one full day a month and two to three days a year to thinking about his organisation; otherwise he would be simply caught up with the immediate and do nothing of any lasting value.[4]

It was Socrates who famously said that 'the unexamined life is not worth living'. If you are spending time with God, that will help you do that appropriate examination, but why not give your thinking that kind of priority? Who knows what ideas and initiatives are waiting for you, if you would only give yourself some space? Leading like Jesus will mean thinking in the ways that He thought about His world.

Renewed thinking – part of discipleship

We have noted that a Christian is someone who is following Jesus. We follow Jesus by hearing and obeying His teaching, and therefore, by definition, we reject other ways of looking at life. Paul, when writing to the Romans, says:

'Therefore, I urge you, brothers and sisters, in view of
God's mercy, to offer your bodies as a living
sacrifice, holy and pleasing to God – this is your true
and proper worship. Do not conform to the pattern of
this world, but be transformed by the renewing of your
mind.' (Rom. 12:1–2)

The pattern of this world is contrasted with the life of God. We are journeying with Jesus in changing from one lifestyle to another. When writing to the Ephesians, Paul explains how renewing the mind comes about:

'You were taught, with regard to your former way of life,
to put off your old self, which is being corrupted by its
deceitful desires; to be made new in the attitude of
your minds; *and to put on the new self, created to be*
like God in true righteousness and holiness.'
(Eph. 4:22–24, emphasis added)

The 'hinge' between our old behaviour and the new, is our *renewed minds*. Some translations say 'spirit' of the mind, to convey the unseen but powerful work on the mind that the believer experiences. A little earlier on in his letter to the Ephesians, Paul wrote this:

'So I tell you this, and insist on it in the Lord, that you
must no longer live as the Gentiles do, in the futility of
their thinking. They are darkened in their
understanding and separated from the life of God
because of the ignorance that is in them due to the
hardening of their hearts.' (Eph. 4:17–18)

Some believe that temptation to sin (or, in the worst cases, abandoning the right to lead) comes because of bodily desire. We forget that most sin starts in the *mind*. We 'decide' God cannot meet our needs and we need to go outside His loving parameters.

But Paul is contrasting those who live according to the values that are regarded as 'normal' in the world (which supports and encourages our various appetites to be fulfilled), and those who have put on 'the new self', where God is at work (which is something we do in harmony with – and dependence on – the Spirit). Paul later continues: 'That, however, is not the way of life you learned when you heard about Christ and were taught in him in accordance with the truth that is in Jesus' (Eph. 4:20–21).

At times it was necessary for the apostles to remind us that godly thinking is not automatic. Take a look at the following scriptures addressed to Christians:

> *'Brothers and sisters, stop thinking like children. In*
> *regard to evil be infants, but in your thinking be adults.'*
> (1 Cor. 14:20)

> *'All of us also lived among them at one time, gratifying*
> *the cravings of our flesh and following its desires*
> *and thoughts. Like the rest, we were by nature*
> *deserving of wrath.'* (Eph. 2:3)

> *'have you not discriminated among yourselves and*
> *become judges with evil thoughts?'* (James 2:4)

The Christian leader, learning from Jesus how to lead others, needs their thinking to be renewed by God's truth if their life and ministry are to impact others beneficially. The question is: who is influencing us that we may influence others?

In chapter two we considered the value of certain spiritual practices. In particular, a mind that is filled the Word of God (as a result of regular reading and meditation) will help you adopt a mindset that follows the road less travelled.

As a leader, you may find your thoughts are not in keeping with leading like Jesus. Do the following ring any bells?

Things will never change.

I am no good at this.

God isn't interested.

Something will go wrong that I can't handle.

I need to control things to be successful.

If we are to lead like Jesus, we need to replace such views with His truth. The apostle Paul was aware of the thought battle we face:

> 'For though we live in the world, we do not wage war as the world does. The weapons we fight with are not the weapons of the world. On the contrary, they have divine power to demolish strongholds. We demolish arguments and every pretension that sets itself up against the knowledge of God, and we take captive every thought to make it obedient to Christ.' (2 Cor. 10:3–5, emphasis added)

Paul knew that, in the words of Bill Johnson, 'We can't afford to have a thought in our heads, that is not in His!' Paul worked to make sure that thoughts were sifted and replaced according to how Jesus sees things.

A tool that helps us to do this is the ABC model, developed by psychologist Albert Ellis.[5] An apparently neutral event will be interpreted differently according to the perspectives of those viewing the event. In Ellis' ABC model:

A = Activating event

B = Belief

C = Consequent emotion

What we believe about an event will lead to the consequent emotion. You can only get to C from A via B. As an example, imagine you are walking down the street and see someone you know. They ignore you. If you believe they have done so deliberately, you feel shunned and annoyed. But if you believe that they are upset or distracted, you will feel nothing yourself – and may in fact feel sad for them. These are two completely different emotional responses from the same 'activating event', based on two different beliefs.

Ellis' model has since been developed. You can add a 'D' and 'E' – 'D' to dispute the belief, and 'E' to signify a changed emotion. Those with troubling emotions therefore have the opportunity to rethink their beliefs about it.

As Christians, we have the power within us to live godly lives, if we choose to fix our thoughts in the right place. We can waste unnecessary time wondering where thoughts have come from. The enemy of our souls can apparently play on our thoughts. In Matthew 16:23, we read how Jesus turned and said to Peter, 'Get behind me, Satan! You are a stumbling block to me; you do not have in mind the concerns of God, but merely human concerns.' This seems to imply that Peter's words were from the enemy.

We also know that our sinful nature will lead us away from godly thinking. Where negative thinking comes from need not especially concern us – we replace the bad with the good as we reflect on Scripture, which gives us God's view of the world.

Expanded vision

Scripture is an assured route to hearing God and thinking God's thoughts after Him. But we need God's Spirit to help us in our interpretation, to sense the areas of His truth that are especially applicable and to direct us in areas that are not directly addressed in Scripture. Thinking like Jesus involves us, on occasion, knowing what He knows and is willing to reveal to us.[6] God has things to say about your leadership – if only you would give Him space to speak! I once heard John Mark Comer (New Wine) speak of learning to live in two places at once. I like this perspective. You live as a leader, but maintain an ear for what God may say in any situation.

Spending time in prayer and Bible study helps us appreciate the bigness of God. One particular example that springs to mind comes from the experience of Bruce Collins who, after a ministry visit to Kenya, was left with a burden for the impoverishment of the farms, which were yielding pitiful produce – causing many of the farmers to search for more income in local towns.

On the radio, Bruce shared how he sensed God saying, '*You give them something to eat*', from Jesus' words to His disciples just before He fed the five thousand. Bruce had no idea how this might be accomplished, but over a few years of investigation and prayer was led to create agricultural schools to train the local farmers in better techniques that would better utilise the natural environment. He set up a charity called Just Earth, and now 2,200 farmers have been trained, yields are up six times in average, and there's interest from the Kenyan Agriculture Minister who wishes to apply this approach elsewhere. Farmers no longer need to leave home to find work in local towns, and children with more than one meal a day are able to concentrate better. Bruce takes his own human efforts, combines them with God's, and they do great things!

Involving God will start with a prayer that goes something like this: 'God, I can't lead this in a way that pleases You and gives You room. Help me to see what You are doing, and to co-operate so that glory may go to You.'

It may be that it is easier to see this applied to leading a church or charity, but any leader can participate in this kingdom work. Christ will give wisdom to the labourer in a commercial enterprise or government department, just as He will a pastor in a church or the director of a charity.

The apostle Paul says: 'And whatever you do, whether in word or deed, do it all in the name of the Lord Jesus, giving thanks to God the Father through him' (Col. 3:17). Think about your leading. Can you do it in the name of Jesus? If you can, then apply those verses from John 15:16: 'You did not choose me, but I chose you and appointed you so that you might go and bear fruit – fruit that will last – and so that whatever you ask in my name the Father will give you.'

Clive Doubleday was the leader of a Baptist church in Kent, when the crisis in Kosova hit the news headlines in 1999. Moved by the reported suffering, he was able to collect bags full of clothes, blankets and toiletries – and with his wife, Ruth, took two lorries to Macedonia. In September 1999, Clive and Ruth concluded their ministry at their church in Kent and started a charity called Smile International to help make a difference to those in need. From these relatively small beginnings, the charity has expanded, providing aid to the poor in Africa, Asia and other parts of Europe, offering opportunities for many Christians to serve as volunteers in alleviating poverty and bringing the good news of God's love to people everywhere. This was a man who allowed God to expand his vision beyond the immediate need he saw, and trusted God to open the doors to help more people.

Even a Christian leader operating in a context where there is little or no apparent faith agenda can still pray that God would bless his or her actions. God may prosper Christian leaders who serve Him faithfully – as a blessing to them, and as a testimony to those who look on and might get to know Him for themselves.

Great expectations

Educators seem fond of this particular story. In 1964, researcher Robert Rosenthal and his colleagues tested every pupil at Oak Elementary School in the southern San Francisco Unified School District. They used a test that pretended to predict academic 'blooming'. Then they gave each teacher the names of a few children from their classroom that would, according to the test, 'bloom' in the school year ahead. In reality, though, the names of the 'bloomers' were randomly selected. The bloomers did not know that the teachers were holding high expectations of them, and the teachers were told not to tell them either. So the children never knew. The bloomers weren't any smarter than their peers – the difference was in the minds of their teachers.

Can you predict what happened? A year later, when the kids were tested again, they found that the bloomers had shown greater intellectual gains than the other pupils. The children actually got smarter when they were *expected* to get smarter by their teachers. They were transformed by their teachers' expectations.[7] Renewing our thinking is a crucial part of walking the leadership road less travelled. This kind of academic study confirms what the Bible tells us about thinking and beliefs.

It is my belief that many Christians in leadership have a mindset that fails to live in the good of all that Jesus promises. Rather than 'Do great things', their motto would be, 'Attempt to get by as best you can'.

Whatever you are doing in leadership, ask yourself – are you asking big things of God that He may get glory from your efforts? This is the road less travelled, and too often, I haven't walked down it. Instead, I've often allowed small-minded thinking to permeate my view. I am relieved that I have preached a sermon, rather than looking expectantly for what God has done. I am relieved that we have enough people to run the course, rather than looking to God to ask that we might be overflowing with attendees.

Perhaps you are the same? Do you sometimes fall into the trap of assuming that God must want yours to always be a small church, or that your charity is better running out of a living room with no staff, or that you can work best as a leader in a company if you are not too successful? Consequently, do you pray, 'Lord help me get by' prayers, expecting very little of God and yourself?

But we can pray bigger prayers! Craig Groeschel says that when he started Life Church Online, it was a really big deal for them to set the goal of reaching 1,000 people. But now they reach 40,000 – and are imagining even bigger goals. UK church life might seem worlds away from that, but Craig is walking the leadership road less travelled, praying big prayers that God's name would be known through his efforts. Maybe it's time you and I did the same.

....

Questions to consider

- What tools (or activities) do you have in place to ensure your mindset is healthy?
- Who can you learn from who will stretch your thinking on leadership?
- Who can you meet with that will give you a mental boost?

8. Handling opposition

'Remember what I told you: "A servant is not greater than his master." If they persecuted me, they will persecute you also. If they obeyed my teaching, they will obey yours also.' (John 15:20)

I was reading the Gospels while preparing a course I run at CWR, called 'The Life and Times of Jesus'. I had assumed that the opposition Jesus faced came mostly as He visited Jerusalem in that final week, and had pretty vehement interaction with the religious authorities before being finally arrested, sentenced and executed. But in my reading I discovered that all the way through His public ministry, Jesus was opposed.

In fact, opposition of some kind is mentioned fairly early on in each of the Gospels. In Matthew, we have Herod trying to kill Jesus before He is out of nappies. A few chapters later, Jesus heals two demon-possessed men in the region of the Gadarenes, and read that the villagers 'pleaded with him to leave their region' (Matt. 8:34). After healing the man with the withered hand, we read in Mark's Gospel that 'the Pharisees went out and began to plot with the Herodians how they might kill Jesus' (Mark 3:6). It gets pretty heated in the Luke's account of Jesus reading from the Scriptures at His local synagogue in Nazareth: 'All the people in the synagogue were furious... They got up, drove him out of the town, and took him to the brow of the hill... in order to throw him off the cliff' (Luke 4:28–29). And in his Gospel, John writes: 'because Jesus was doing these things on the Sabbath, the Jewish leaders began to persecute him' (John 5:16). In John 8, they even tried to stone Him.

It became clear to me that there were parallel things going on in the Gospels: a warming to Jesus by many, including large crowds hearing His message, but at the same time, opposition from the very start to what He was doing and saying that contravened the Jewish leaders' sensibilities. This would be a brewing storm throughout Jesus' public ministry that would break during that last week.

As we have seen, the leadership road less travelled is centred on the idea that we are led in the way of Christ by the power of the Spirit. It's quite likely, therefore, that we will find opposition in some way. As Jesus says to His disciples:

'If they persecuted me, they will persecute you also.
If they obeyed my teaching, they will obey yours also.'
(John 15:20)

But there's a reason why we're calling this the road *less* travelled. I'm not going to suggest that putting these ideas into practice will be a smooth process. Let's assume for a moment that you accept the premises of this book, that Christ calls you to a better way of leading and you look to be more open to the Holy Spirit. As you start to change, you will immediately discover where the opposition is going to come from.

Opposition from fellow leaders

I once heard a Christian missionary report back from a trip to an island off the coast of Scotland. When speaking about the lack of progress in the things of God, he referred to 'tall poppy syndrome'. Just as tall poppies are cut back, so anyone who seeks to go further with God receives the response: 'who do you think you are?'

Inevitably, any change or growth may receive a similar kind of remark or attitude. It comes to the young man who gets excited about his faith and wants to be involved in outreach in a resistant church; it comes to the woman who discovers God for the first time and likes to raise hands in worship in a congregation that would normally prefer a less expressive stance. It comes to the boss who realises that some of his company's practices are not ethical and sets about changing them.

There are a number of things going on: jealousy at what you have been shown, or at what has happened; fear, that maybe they will have to change; embarrassment, they know you are correct but don't want to admit it; annoyance, that your change is an implied criticism of them.

If you take your cues from fellow leaders and not from God,

you will probably buckle under the peer pressure (or you'll say nothing, because you already know what they will say).

Any change or growth *may* lead to negative feedback, but it also *may not*. In some leadership teams, any sharing of new approaches is accepted. It would be sad to assume there's a problem that doesn't actually exist. If you share what you now believe with all due humility and generosity to those who may think differently, you have the chance to enter into genuine dialogue that can help you and them.

Opposition from those opposed to change

Bruce Collins was a London-based Anglian rector who I interviewed on the topic of transition. He had seen God equip people through His Spirit, and wanted to see this happen where he served. Bruce believed that most churches are made up of four categories of people when it comes to change:

The radicals (often young people) – they will run through a brick wall if you invite them to.

The progressives (often the parents of the young people) – they will eventually go through the hole in the wall but try and tidy it up.

The conservatives (could be any age) – they are not sure that they would ever want to make a hole at all.

The traditionalists (tend to be older) – they have an emotional attachment to past ways of doing things. Get them on side and they are very happy for holes to be made in walls, as long as it doesn't involve them.

According to Bruce, only the first group would demonstratively be with you if you wanted to make a change in the church; the other three would need careful managing. He told me: 'We had a traditional group who were very happy for me to change the morning service, just as long as their early morning Communion stayed. Indeed – in time, they were some of my biggest supporters because I had respected their wishes.'

You may find that you are able to make changes to your leading 'over time'. You may be opposed, but not forever – if you allow people to understand. Bruce introduced teaching on the Holy Spirit that the progressives were able to embrace, because they had been convinced through the Scriptures that this was the way ahead. You may find that those who initially oppose you will come round, if you give them time. The irony is, however, that change should be the normal Christian life. We are all in a process of growing, and so should ideally be aware of the need to rethink life in the light of what we now know.

Opposition from the enemy

We know we have a real spiritual foe who is out to see us taken down. For some Christian leaders, this opposition is literally life-threatening. One such example is that of Canon Andrew White. I had the privilege of interviewing Andrew a year or so prior to him becoming the 'Vicar of Baghdad' in 2005. At the time, he was then Director of International Ministry at the International Centre for Reconciliation at Coventry Cathedral, England. I had the opportunity to join a three-day tour he led to Jerusalem, which included a 'surprise' visit to Yasser Arafat, former chairman of the Palestine Liberation Organisation, who was under house arrest in a former police station in Ramallah. This was when the United States was not 'officially' talking to him, but apparently used Andrew as an 'unofficial' go-between. Andrew was one of the very few to be respected by both Palestinians and Israelis. On the back of this trip, he kindly agreed to be my guest on radio. Having been diagnosed with multiple sclerosis aged 33, just after starting his reconciliation work, I asked him how he manages with his punishing schedule. 'The grace of God,' came his impassioned reply. And that's all he would say! (Though he did add that his MS seems to be better when he is busy.)

Andrew was dubbed 'Vicar of Baghdad' because his church – St George's Church, Baghdad – was the only Anglican church in Iraq. But it also fitted his larger-than-life persona. His profile reads like scenes from an episode of the TV series *24*: he has been hijacked, kidnapped, held at gunpoint, and locked in rooms where people have been tortured. Many of his staff have been killed – including 11 staff in just one year. As pastor of his flock, he would baptise new believers, aware that their decision to follow Jesus made them targets, and many would pay for their newfound faith with their life. Eventually, security concerns led the Archbishop of Canterbury to insist that Andrew leave Iraq. Here was a man prepared to die in his service as a leader, and who grieves for the nation of Iraq and all it has been through. He has often said that he would be bored if he had continued in the London church where he was a curate, and I am sure he has loved the adventure, even as he has lost himself in it.

Hopefully you won't receive that level of spiritual opposition. But don't be surprised when some comes, perhaps from the least likely source.

Opposition from ourselves

Our biggest problem when it comes to opposition is ourselves. Yes – that's right! We know this on a personal change level. The apostle Paul articulates the life of the believer:

> '*I do not understand what I do. For what I want to do I do not do, but what I hate I do. And if I do what I do not want to do, I agree that the law is good. As it is, it is no longer I myself who do it, but it is sin living in me. For I know that good itself does not dwell in me, that is, in my sinful nature. For I have the desire to do what is good, but I cannot carry it out. For I do not do the good I want to do, but the evil I do not want to do – this I*

keep on doing. Now if I do what I do not want to do, it is no longer I who do it, but it is sin living in me that does it.' (Rom. 7:15–20)

Doesn't that also describe changes in the way we lead?! For me, it was clear God was challenging me to be less scripted in my sermons, but whenever it came to preach, I would bottle it and take a fully scripted sermon into the pulpit once more. I would preach a couple of times a term in my home church, as well as a few sermons elsewhere, all in addition to the day courses I was teaching at CWR.

If you do any public speaking, you will know there is a balance to be struck between thinking carefully about what you want to say, and having the greater spontaneity that comes from being able to eyeball the congregation. I had been so scripted that I'd lost the potential connection – even if the actual words were well received. I resisted the sense that I really ought to bite the bullet (and use notes instead of a full script) for over a year before finally, one Sunday morning, I went with just an outline.

The vicar had led the service, and would typically be fairly positive afterwards. But that morning, he was unusually effusive. 'That was great!' he said. 'What happened? It seemed to come alive, and you were so expressive!'

I was able to share something of my change of approach, and silently thanked God that I had at last got round to doing what He had been asking.

You too will be the biggest barrier to your own growth. Sometimes it will be sin. CWR founder Selwyn Hughes once said that at the root of all sin is the belief that God cannot be trusted. We are tempted to use our leadership power to get our way; we succumb to the view that if we only had more money, we would be OK. We entertain sexual fantasies with people we know and ones we don't. Each time, we are basically saying: 'God, I don't trust you to come through for me – I need this thought pattern instead.' And of course each of those steps is the first on the road to bullying and manipulation, making our salary an idol, and entertaining extra-marital relationships.

Why do we oppose ourselves? The truth is that the mind can be convinced something is true or good, but feelings can't. Deep down, the desires are still awakened for fulfilment in a different way than God directs. It has been said that feelings are 20 times stronger than thoughts – so it can take a while for us to get to the point where we really believe what we say we believe, and therefore act upon it.

Perhaps deep down we don't believe we deserve the good that would come to us if we acted as we know we should. We sabotage the situation, preferring to wallow in lack than enjoy the abundance, like the teenager who doesn't turn up to the date with the beautiful girl or handsome guy, because they are frightened of blowing it.

So how should we respond to opposition?

1. Recognise who's behind it

John reminds us: 'We know that we are children of God, and that the whole world is under the control of the evil one' (1 John 5:19). It is a sad fact of history – from the beginning of time – that the ways of God will be opposed. If God was to create beings who could freely choose to love and trust Him, then the opposite must also be possible. And so from the time that Adam and Eve disobeyed God, there have always been challenges to God's rule and reign.

We delight at the Old Testament stories, but what were the stories of Moses and the Red Sea, Joshua and the battle of Jericho, Sampson and Delilah, David and Goliath, Elijah and the prophets of Baal, Daniel and the lion's den, and Esther and Haman *actually* about? At their root, someone wanted to oppose the people of God.

God had promised that from Abraham's line all the nations would be blessed – and so it was paramount that the nation survive. So Paul would remind the Ephesians:

'For our struggle is not against flesh and blood, but against the rulers, against the authorities, against the powers of this dark world and against the spiritual forces of evil in the heavenly realms.' (Eph. 6:12)

I am not saying that everyone who opposes you is of the devil or infected by demons, but that we are all subject to an environment that opposes God and are sometimes complicit within it ourselves.

So you don't need to necessarily evaluate opposition and conclude that it is some kind of satanic plot, but you do need to know that such is life that things will drift away from truth and righteousness. If you are coming in and seeking to walk the ways of Jesus, you may bump into the enemy walking the other way. Indeed – it has been said that if you are not receiving any opposition, it may be that you and he are walking in the same direction.

Without going off on one about Satan, we know of course that we have authority against him. He may have power, but he has to submit to that of Jesus – to whom *all* authority has been given. Paul tells us to put on the full armour of God so that we can take our stand against the devil's schemes (Eph. 6:10–17). The armour Paul described, based on the image of the Roman soldier, is based on our faith in the finished work of Christ (breastplate of righteousness, sword of truth, helmet of salvation, shield of faith, shoes of the gospel of peace). I am not sure we are meant to push the image as far as some preachers do, but what is clear is that the merit of Christ means we hold strong.

2. Adjust where you need to

Occasionally, opposition is healthy. It can strengthen our resolve, but also help us. Every criticism has a grain of truth in it. It helps us see how others perceive us and evaluate things. For example, you may have thought that the group you are leading was flexible; their opposition proves they aren't as flexible as you thought.

It is a good rule of Christian leadership to adopt the 'beta model mentality'. The beta model mentality says: 'We are experimenting; this may not work. Come and see and help us improve things.' It's how the Alpha course started out – originally run by Charles Marnham in 1977, and refined and adjusted by Nicky Gumbel when he joined the staff at Holy Trinity Brompton in 1986. As another example, look at Saddleback Valley Community Church – a church of 20,000 plus, which had met in 70 locations in 17 years before finding a permanent home in Lake Forest Orange County in 1992. Their unofficial motto was, 'You can attend – if you can find us!'

There's no reason why you shouldn't see your leadership change as a 'beta change'. See what God is in, listen to critics, and take what you think is the best from what they say.

3. Speak out when you need to

Of all the leaders I have interviewed, perhaps the person who underwent the biggest change in thinking was church pastor Mike Riches. He served at a suburban church in Tacoma, Washington, 32 miles southwest of Seattle. They sensed a move of God and changed from being a church that was conservative in theology to being one more open to the Holy Spirit (often characterised as 'charismatic'). This particular church established a reputation locally for its fast-growing attendance, with significant growth over the previous seven years from 170 to 1,500 plus. When God started moving (Mike Riches' words) in late January 2000, Mike and the leadership team returned to the Bible to consider the implications of what was going on.[1] They determined to be open to what God was doing, and despite the open discussions and Bible teaching explaining the way they believed God was leading them as a church, around 70% of those who were part of the fellowship in 2000 went on to leave. Can you imagine losing 70% of your congregation? Changing thinking has consequences. (What was ironic was that a respected member of staff was healed from a life-threatening condition: people were pleased for him, but still left the church as they didn't have a place in their minds for that kind of supernatural activity.) But over time, attendance grew again and the church was able to reach people who might not have come had they kept to their more conservative approach.

The church where I was Assistant Minister had a rich heritage of Bible teaching through the ministry of Francis W. Dixon, whose ministry put Lansdowne Baptist Church on the map. Among his innovations was the introduction of a 'dial-a-message' ministry. One of my jobs as Assistant Minister was to change the tape so that people could hear him speak when they phoned a particular number, though he had gone to glory some 20 years prior. What may not have been obvious to those attending the church in its heyday, when there would be 600 plus gathering, was that when Francis arrived, the church membership plummeted from 50 to 17, following his decision to dispense with the services of the choir during his first year as the pastor. For him, the road less travelled meant tackling a divisive – in this case, cancerous – problem in the life of the church. It took courage, but subsequent history vindicated his stance.

If God has clearly spoken about how you are leading or what you are doing, your job is to obey, and leave the consequences to Him.

4. Seek peace where you can

If my illustrations have seemed adversarial, it doesn't mean it's the only outcome. Victor Jack, an evangelist in Suffolk, was once my radio guest speaking specifically about handling opposition. He shared the story of the days when he used a large tent for 'crusades' (as they were then known). The tent would be erected on the village green to attract people to come and hear the preacher. Victor was worshipping at a Brethren church at the time, and received quite some opposition from someone who really wasn't a fan of these events – which, to him, were new-fangled means of evangelism

– and he said so. Victor told me how he visited him to resolve the disagreement and repair their relationship – a reconciliation that was especially poignant with the man's death shortly after.

The apostle Paul urges us to 'maintain the unity of the Spirit' for the common good. You will meet with believers who don't see what you see and take umbrage at you. Some may have heard lies about you, or interpreted things in a certain way. But your role is to recognise that the Holy Spirit lives in them, as He does with you. You may agree to differ, but you don't need to break fellowship over it.

5. Carry on regardless

Of course, there comes a time when you need to carry on with what you need to do, in spite of opposition.

This is Bill Johnson, who made revival his chief focus at Bethel Church, California, and lost 70% of the congregation.

This is Jackie Pullinger, who was convinced God had called her overseas. No mission organisation would take her, so she bought a one-way ticket and trusted God to tell her where to get off the boat.

This is Chuck Smith, who refused to listen to the deacons who wanted the hippies to wear shoes in the church sanctuary, and was part of a revival that sparked the Jesus movement in Calvary Chapel, Los Angeles.

This is Gary Grant, founder of the toy store chain The Entertainer, whose retail locations do not open on Sundays. The business does not sell products with any connection to the occult.

It's the road less travelled and these people walk it, come what may. How about you?

Questions to consider

- Where does your opposition typically come from?
- Who normally wins?
- Are you comfortable with how things are with respect to opposition? What can you do to change things?

9. Arriving at your destination

'I press on towards the goal to win the prize for which God has called me heavenward in Christ Jesus.' (Phil. 3:14)

I was with some church leaders one Saturday morning, reflecting on their progress in discipleship as a church. My friend and I had been asked to meet with them to lead a workshop, and I knew the next ten minutes might be interesting. My co-presenter, Hugo Anson, had taken us through Matthew 28 and the Great Commission, where Jesus gives His followers the mandate to make disciples. We had just looked at the various activities that the church was engaged with, which included the standard Sunday services, children and youth activities. Hugo then said, 'So looking back on, say, the last ten years as a church, how many disciples have you made?'[1]

Initially, the room was silent. Then, slowly, a few suggestions were made: names of people who had begun to attend church as a result of Alpha; in one case, because of the Boys' Brigade, a whole family had started coming. But it clearly wasn't a question they often considered.

I have spared the details of the church, not least because it would be very unfair to single them out. In my experience, very few think in these terms. The 'ABC' of church life (Attendance, Buildings, Cash) has supplanted the 'D' and 'E' of the Church: Discipleship and Evangelism (and of course Jesus didn't mention any of the first three in His command!).

Now the whole business of measurement in Christian life is contentious. Wasn't David judged by God for counting his troops? Aren't we wrong to attempt to quantify the work of God? Where in the New Testament is there any mention of the size of a church? Was the church in Thessalonica bigger than the one in Philippi? Was the church in Colossae bigger than that in Ephesus? We don't know. We guess that the churches were no bigger than the large dwellings of that day – which, with a courtyard arrangement, might accommodate around 50 – but we just don't know. It's clear that Scripture is silent on the matter. It's not something we need to know.

Anyone who operates in a world of 'artificial metrics' will be aghast at the thought of such methods being applied to Christian leading. For example, a school may do poorly on numbers of pupils accomplishing

GCSE passes, but have done incredibly well given the challenges that a cohort of children presented, and better than a school that had better academic results but saw smaller improvements. Similarly, how do we measure the disciple-making capacity of a church in an area that has an ethnic population connected to other religions, versus one that has a residual Christian understanding? One has ripe fruit to pick, the other is barren land with little seed sown.

But away from the Church world, where metrics may be hard to set, what of the leadership road less travelled? How might we ever say we have arrived at our destination? How might you measure how you are doing as a leader in a factory, or a shop, a successful company or a government department? The industry may have its metrics to do with income and staff turnover, or claims processed or products launched, but this is hardly appropriate here. How do you measure your leading as a Christian?

Let's look again at the Bible. Is measurement absent?

In Exodus, specific people are evacuated from Egypt. Later, the names of the tribes who entered the Promised Land are listed. In Judges, we have accounts of battles including details of the miniscule number of troops used to defeat Midian under Gideon. In 1 and 2 Samuel and 1 and 2 Kings, we have accounts of more battles won and lost, with details of the size of the troops and the enemy, including the 185,000 Assyrians struck dead in one night. We have tales of the Exile of Israel and Judah, and precise names of those who would eventually return. We have Nehemiah rebuilding the wall in 52 days, and Haggai urging the rebuilding of the Temple.

In the New Testament, we have 12 apostles and the feeding of the 5,000 (and indeed the 4,000). We have 120 in the upper room and 3,000 and then 5,000 coming to faith. We have the news that a few people responded when Paul preached in Athens, including the name of Damaris.

I could go on. My point? There is some evaluation of leadership activity in Scripture. In David's case, the numbering was probably to do with his pride in treating the people as if they were 'his' to number, when they were God's people. That's why he was judged.

This doesn't invalidate membership lists and parish electoral rolls and knowing who attended Alpha last Monday. (Indeed, I know one minister of a sizeable church who knows exactly who attended small group in the previous week!) And nor does it stop us from asking hard questions of our lives and what we seek to achieve as Christian leaders. The title of this chapter alludes to the end of life's journey, but also to those points on the way, where we accomplish tasks and projects as leaders. The leadership road less travelled means some appropriate assessment of things, from time to time, so that we can know where we are on the leadership journey and when and whether it is time for us to move to something else. This is surely leading as God intends us to.

How many times has God said to a group of people: 'Plant a church in that part of town, but don't expect anyone to attend'? How many times has He met with a business leader and said, 'I expect you to have zero influence with your colleagues'? Or with a mum, 'Your children will drift away from faith in their teens, so why bother?'? God looks for outcomes from our leading. I want to look at two key areas that flow from the leadership road less travelled: behaviour (the way of Christ) and fruit (the power of the Spirit).

Behaviour

What we do flows from who we are. We might like to think a particular behaviour is 'out of character' or 'that wasn't me'. But the truth is that what we do is a reflection of something going on within. Jesus says: 'For out of the heart come evil thoughts – murder, adultery, sexual immorality, theft, false testimony, slander' (Matt. 15:19). Throughout the New Testament there is teaching that suggests behaviour patterns for believers, both positive and negative:

'The acts of the flesh are obvious: sexual immorality,
impurity and debauchery; idolatry and witchcraft; hatred,
discord, jealousy, fits of rage, selfish ambition, dissensions,
factions and envy; drunkenness, orgies, and the like.
I warn you, as I did before, that those who live like this
will not inherit the kingdom of God.' (Gal. 5:19–21)

It goes without saying that, as a leader, you will be wanting to avoid this kind of stuff. Paul is pretty explicit in his claims that those who live like this are not going to inherit the kingdom, by which I understand that a lifestyle of indulging this kind of behaviour is indicative of someone not on the road with God.

There are other lists in Colossians 3:5–10 and 1 Timothy 1:9–11 that also give us insights. The point is not to have a mental checklist of sins, but to note the range of behaviour issues that are contrary to a walk with the Spirit, and seek to walk *in* the Spirit, cultivating the kind of lifestyle that reflects the Spirit within.

In his first letter to the Corinthians, Paul implies that the believers to whom he wrote were 'immature':

'Brothers and sisters, I could not address you as people
who live by the Spirit but as people who are still worldly
– mere infants in Christ. I gave you milk, not solid food,
for you were not yet ready for it. Indeed, you are still not
ready. You are still worldly. For since there is jealousy
and quarrelling among you, are you not worldly? Are
you not acting like mere humans? For when one says,
"I follow Paul," and another, "I follow Apollos," are you
not mere human beings?' (1 Cor. 3:1–4)

Paul does not expand here at any length, but implies that some behaviour is 'worldly' and reflects their state as 'mere human beings', which suggests that he is expecting a level of maturity that reflects the Spirit's work. Interestingly, this church was one that had seen a high level of supernatural activity (perhaps more than most churches in the UK would be used to?), but was still described as 'worldly'. The implication from the lists of sins and vices in Paul's epistles is that such behaviour needed to change if the believers were to 'mature'.

Let's look at an intriguing passage in Hebrews. The author implies that certain kinds of teaching that leads to activity is foundational:

> *'Therefore let us move beyond the elementary teachings about Christ and be taken forward to maturity, not laying again the foundation of repentance from acts that lead to death, and of faith in God, instruction about cleansing rites, the laying on of hands, the resurrection of the dead, and eternal judgment. And God permitting, we will do so.'* (Heb. 6:1–3)

The writer is addressing those who had come from a Jewish background, hence the mention of instruction about cleansing rites (not an issue that typically concerns recent converts in the towns and cities of the UK), so our application will need to consider the original context. But it is useful to note that the author has in mind some 'elementary teachings of Christ', and that these included 'the laying on of hands' – which, in most UK churches, is something regarded as being for the more spiritually mature.

When writing to Christians in Galatia, Paul is concerned that his readers grow: 'My dear children, for whom I am again in the pains of childbirth until Christ is formed in you' (Gal. 4:19). He felt pain because he knew that the church was not, on the whole, in a good place. But positively, Paul tells us:

> *'But the fruit of the Spirit is love, joy, peace, forbearance, kindness, goodness, faithfulness, gentleness and self-control. Against such things there is no law.'* (Gal. 5:22–23)

If you sense these character qualities developing over time as you put yourself in the way of God's grace, through practising the ways of Jesus – that's a cause for rejoicing! Peter, too, speaks of some sort of progression, even if it's not clear that one follows from another:

> *'For this very reason, make every effort to add to your faith goodness; and to goodness, knowledge; and to knowledge, self-control; and to self-control, perseverance; and to perseverance, godliness; and to godliness, mutual affection; and to mutual affection, love. For if you possess these qualities in increasing measure, they will keep you from being ineffective and unproductive in your knowledge of our Lord Jesus Christ. But whoever does not have them is near sighted and blind, forgetting that they have been cleansed from their past sins.'* (2 Pet. 1:5–9)

Peter knew that believers would be wanting to see all these qualities. Indeed, lacking these qualities was a sign that we have forgotten that our sins have been dealt with.

Our purpose for highlighting this is that those writing the New Testament had an idea of what following Jesus looked like, and weren't afraid to label some behaviour as unacceptable or immature, and other behaviour as befitting those who know they are in Christ. The epistles were partly written because the believers were struggling in some way. The apostles did not shrug their shoulders and say a prayer; they did what they could to help, which in some cases was write (all Paul could do anyway as he spent time in prison).

If you are battling with some of these 'sins' or areas of maturity, you won't need me to highlight them. We note things not to become morose, but to highlight in prayer what we want the Lord to be at work in so that we can see change, and see our capacity to assist others with integrity grow.

Fruit

I understand that John Wimber, founder of Vineyard Church, took seven months. Evangelist Todd White speaks of taking four. Bill Johnson, Senior Pastor of Bethel Church, doesn't give a timeline other than it was 'a considerable time'. Chris Gore, also of Bethel, writes of a thousand prayers.

I am referring to the length of time that passed between their first prayers for healing, and actually seeing someone healed! There came a point when each saw an increase in the measure in which God was at work in their prayers.

'Fruit' is how the outcomes of faith are often described. (I appreciate that character and behaviour are also described in this way too. These are not in mind here.) When Jesus spent extended time with His followers before He ascended to heaven, giving them some closing directions as the time came for him to leave the earth, He said:

> 'Believe me when I say that I am in the Father and the
> Father is in me; or at least believe on the evidence of the
> works themselves. Very truly I tell you, whoever
> believes in me will do the works I have been doing, and
> they will do even greater things than these, because I
> am going to the Father. And I will do whatever you
> ask in my name, so that the Father may be glorified in
> the Son.' (John 14:11–13)

In what is commonly known as the 'upper room discourse' (John 14–17), Jesus included instructions of where He was going and the anticipation of the gift of the Holy Spirit who would be present in their lives. He also said these astonishing words about their relationship with God and what He would do for them. Jesus told the Twelve (and those who would believe in the future) that they would do *greater works* than Him when He left earth. This comes as a surprise, for no one has lived as Jesus lived, and so there is a lot of speculation about this. Does this mean 'greater' in terms of quantity – because He anticipates the disciples ministering for many years, seeing more people healed than He had in His three-year ministry? We don't know for sure. But the rest of the passage includes the promise that we can ask for things in His name, and the Father will do it – a promise repeated in John 15:7–8,16:

> *'If you remain in me and my words remain in you, ask whatever you wish, and it will be done for you. This is to my Father's glory, that you bear much fruit, showing yourselves to be my disciples… You did not choose me, but I chose you and appointed you so that you might go and bear fruit – fruit that will last – and so that whatever you ask in my name the Father will give you.'*

Whether John 14:11 refers to miracles or not, the promise is that we may ask in Jesus' name for anything, that God may be glorified. It is my belief that many Christians in leadership have a mindset that fails to live in the good of all that Jesus promises. Rather than 'do great things', their motto would be 'attempt to get by'.

So, I am asking: what would this kind of fruit look like for you? Would it be people coming to faith through your life and witness? Would it be people being healed through your prayers? Would it be answered prayer with respect to some aspect of your business affairs or charitable endeavours? Would it be steps of faith made within your family? Would it be 'disciples made', as in the story at the start of this chapter?

It seems that fruit matters to Jesus, and can matter to you. What are you going to look for? What will you evaluate? And has there been any change in whatever you are measuring? Might this be significant? Is this an indication of time to adjust what you do, or where you do it? Or is it just one of those things you need to persevere in?

It can be sobering to step back from the busyness of life and ask ourselves: what fruit is developing from what I am doing? But it can be equally thrilling to step off life's treadmill for a while and rejoice in all that God is doing in your life.

I tend to interview people on my radio show because they have seen sizeable fruit – churches that flourish, charities that see progress within their field, ministries that start to make a serious dent in the darkness in which they are shining. Maybe the kind of fruit you will see might create the kind of stories we should feature on the show!

Trust

Having argued that there are some metrics that we can measure, I finish this chapter aware that we also need to measure ourselves in terms of trust. Paul reminded us that we fix our eyes on what is unseen (2 Cor. 4:18). We are to set our minds on things above (Col. 3:2).

Having hopefully convinced you that it is appropriate and wise to do some reflection and measuring of your leading, let me now remind you that there will always be things we cannot know, and have to trust God with. We lead the way we lead because it is the way of the Master.

> *'Very truly I tell you, unless a grain of wheat falls to the ground and dies, it remains only a single seed. But if it dies, it produces many seeds.'* (John 12:24)

We die to self, unsure how God will use what we give. We sow seed in sharing faith. We do secret acts of service. We trust the unseen work of the Spirit. We look forward to the day when what we have sown bears fruit for eternity.

I once had the opportunity to chat with Sandy Millar, then rector of Holy Trinity Brompton, the home of Alpha. I asked him how they evaluate what Alpha is accomplishing, given that they deliberately choose to not follow up those who leave the course. In replying, he referenced one of the parables: 'We leave things, and then every now and again look and see what has grown!'

It was a wise answer. We may measure some things, and I believe we can and should. But ultimately, the road less travelled is one that God evaluates.

I want to underpin all of this with the following passage from 1 Corinthians, and the prayer that we as Christian leaders will build with durable materials.

> 'What, after all, is Apollos? And what is Paul? Only servants, through whom you came to believe – as the Lord has assigned to each his task. I planted the seed, Apollos watered it, but God has been making it grow. So neither the one who plants nor the one who waters is anything, but only God, who makes things grow. The one who plants and the one who waters have one purpose, and they will each be rewarded according to their own labour. For we are co-workers in God's service; you are God's field, God's building.
>
> By the grace God has given me, I laid a foundation as a wise builder, and someone else is building on it. But each one should build with care. For no one can lay any foundation other than the one already laid, which is Jesus Christ. If anyone builds on this foundation using gold, silver, costly stones, wood, hay or straw, their work will be shown for what it is, because the Day will bring it to light. It will be revealed with fire, and the fire will test the quality of each person's work. If what has been built survives, the builder will receive a reward. If it is burned up, the builder will suffer loss but yet will be saved – even though only as one escaping through the flames.' (1 Cor. 3:5–15)

My prayer is that you will have been found to be one whose work endures and is rewarded. The leadership road less travelled has the final destination in heaven itself and meeting Jesus, with whom we have walked by His Spirit, and then face to face. We will be overjoyed to have arrived, and He will be there to greet us and all who have walked this road. He will welcome us to the new heaven and earth, as co-rulers of the next phase of what He has in place. Leading as God intends us to, leads to *more* leading as God intends us to. You are quite literally training for reigning.

May God equip you for everything God He has for you in this journey, at whatever stage you are: whether starting out, on the road a while, or coming to the end. What you do matters to Him, and is a very real part of His unfolding purposes. Walk well.

Questions to consider

- Which of the metrics in this chapter will you be using?
- Are you convinced that measurement is vital?
- What is your prayer regarding this?

10. Deciding your next steps

'Do not merely listen to the word, and so deceive yourselves. Do what it says.'

(James 1:22)

I said in chapter two that there needs to be vision, intention and means for change to take place – and we looked at this in terms of seeing personal character transformation as God works in and through the things we do.

To state things slightly differently, change will take place if:

1. Your mind is convinced it's necessary and possible
2. Your will and emotions come in line
3. You know what actions you need to take.

Miss out on any of these three and lasting change will be hard to sustain. One image that might be helpful here is that of a boy riding an elephant. The boy represents our rational side. We can be convinced through Scripture that the way of Christ really is the one we want. The elephant represents our emotions (appropriately much larger than the boy). If the change doesn't feel like something you really want to do, you will find it hard. Your mind may be convinced, but if you are not moved to change, you will stay stuck. If your mind and emotions are thoroughly convinced, you still need a pathway on which to walk (actions to take).[1]

Have I convinced your mind?

We have seen that Jesus calls us to follow Him, and this is our primary task. As we've said, seeking to be a Christian leader means leading in the way of Jesus in the power of the Spirit. God makes this gloriously possible. People are changing all the time, and God is raising up leaders in all walks of life who are extending His work and seeing extraordinary things done.

How do you feel about this?

Is there a sigh inside you that says, 'Oh boy, this seems like more hard work'? Or, 'I am quite comfortable leading as I lead just now'?

My prayer is that you will ask God for the vision of a new you, and you will understand that though challenging, taking the leadership road less travelled is the very best and (in the right sense of the word) easiest way to live for Christ. Remember that God is involved in the future with you. His intentions are good and He longs to bless you. When Jesus prays to His Father in John 17, He includes an extraordinary statement: He has been praying for His followers, and turns to those who would believe in Him through their message:

> 'My prayer is not for them alone. I pray also for those who will believe in me through their message, that all of them may be one, Father, just as you are in me and I am in you. May they also be in us so that the world may believe that you have sent me. I have given them the glory that you gave me, that they may be one as we are one – I in them and you in me – so that they may be brought to complete unity. Then the world will know that you sent me and have loved them even as you have loved me.' (John 17:20–23)

Note that last sentence: that God loves us *as* He loves His own Son. Wow!

Don't doubt for a moment the love of the Father for you. His grace towards you is immense. So the foundation of any activity on our part is the work of God and His commitment to us, which makes anything we do possible.

So, regarding what we need to do to see change, what exactly will you need to do?

Here's a summary of some of the areas we have considered in the book. Some will be more important to you than others. Look through them prayerfully and commit to the thinking and activity required.

Actions

The key activities that underpin a leadership road less travelled concern the ways we put ourselves in the way of God's grace.

In chapter two, we looked at practising the ways of Jesus and suggested that you intentionally make space for them in your schedule. If you haven't done this already, here's a reminder of things to try to include:

Personal, devotional activities
- Prayer (personal)
- Bible reading
- Study (for a longer period of time)
- Fasting
- Solitude (deliberate times of retreat)
- Meditation

Corporate activities
- Worship
- Celebration (such as meals with friends)
- Corporate prayer (in church, or with one or more prayer partners)
- Bible study (perhaps in a small group)
- Service
- Submission (setting aside time when you consciously allow others to set the agenda)

Identity

We looked at our identity in Christ and the importance of remembering who we are. Here are some questions that you might regularly like to ask yourself:
- How important to you is your role or job title?
- How do you see yourself?
- How do others see you? Is this a challenge to how you should see yourself in Christ?
- You will be playing a role to some extent as you lead, but how good are you at remembering that it's your identity in Christ that matters?

Energy levels

To say it once more: the leadership road less travelled is leading in the way of Christ by the power of the Spirit. If you regularly practise the disciplines above, you are already giving the Holy Spirit room to be at work. Thank Him for all He is doing already, and continue to look to Him for power for service in everything you do, however mundane. Check that you are not grieving or quenching the Spirit. Ask forgiveness if you are, and for a fresh filling.

Joining others

Where we lead can be hostile to what we have considered in this book, and good intentions can be lost when the pressure of co-workers' and fellow leaders' attitudes clash with God's purposes. Make sure you consider:

- Who is walking the leadership road less travelled with you?
- Are there people who might benefit from this book? How about your spouse, or a family member?
- Who might you contact?
- What steps do you need to take to increase your range of connections, that you may receive support?

Finding direction

- Do you know where you are heading? Is it congruent with your gifts, your heart and where you believe God is leading you?
- Do you know why you are leading?
- What is the 'one thing' you need to do today (or this week or this month)?
- How well are you using your diary to focus on your priorities?
- Does your diary reflect the person you want to become?

Your mindset

- Is your thinking fueled by God?
- Consider the input you receive each day. Where does it come from?
- How might you invest better in your thinking? Are there websites you could use? Blogs? Podcasts? Downloads? CDs?
- How big are your expectations and dreams for what God is going to do as you lead? Is it time to pray accordingly?

The opposition

- Where do you sense your greatest opposition to walking this road? Is it from fellow workers? From the enemy, or from yourself?
- How can you overcome it?
- Do you need anyone to help you?

Arrival

- Reflecting on your leading, how do you think you are doing?
- How do those you work with think you are doing? (It may be appropriate to ask!)
- What metrics are you using to assess progress? Are these the correct ones?

Spend time in prayer asking God to reveal what He thinks and where He is looking for you to focus next. Is there any sense of transition in your thinking, a new challenge in the place where you lead, or in a new area? Are there people you need to involve with you in leading, or who need to be empowered to lead themselves?

You have a chance to commit to action.

The leadership road less travelled stretches before you. It's time to take your first steps.

Ready?

Endnotes

Introduction
[1]My radio show, *The Leadership File*, is on Premier Christian Radio every Sunday at 3.30pm. You can listen online at www.premierchristianradio.com or access old shows archived on iTunes.
[2]M. Scott Peck, *The Road Less Travelled* (London: Simon & Schuster, 1997)

Chapter 1
[1]Rob Bell, *Velvet Elvis: Repainting the Christian Faith* (New York: HarperCollins, 2006), p84
[2]God had called them to be a 'kingdom of priests' when He made the covenant at Sinai. Some argue they almost immediately declined, preferring Moses to be their mediator. God set up a 'priesthood' through the tribe of Levi. The northern tribes were exiled to Assyria in 722 BC, never to return. Judah was exiled in 586 BC by the Babylonians, and returned some 70 years later.
[3]Look up 'kingdom' in Elane O'Rourke (Ed.), *A Dallas Willard Dictionary* (Soul Training Publications, 2013)

Chapter 2
[1]For more information, visit www.dwillard.org/articles
[2]Dallas Willard, *Renovation of the Heart: Putting on the Character of Christ* (Colorado Springs, CO, USA: NavPress, 2002), p85
[3]Richard Foster, *The Spiritual Formation Bible* (New York: HarperOne, 2006)
[4] If you want further help for practices in the way of Jesus, I recommend some fantastic free resources by John Mark Comer, available at www.practicingtheway.org
You will get links to explanations of each and how to work through them in small groups.

Chapter 3
[1]Howard Gardner, *Leading Minds* (New York: Basic Books, 2011)
[2]It is widely believed that the apostle Andrew was martyred in Greece in AD 60 by crucifixion, and is reputed to have said: 'I have long desired and expected this happy hour. The cross has been consecrated by the body of Christ hanging on it.'

Chapter 4
[1]Dallas Willard, *The Divine Conspiracy* (San Francisco: HarperSanFrancisco, 1998)

Chapter 5
[1]Isabel Myers had estimated that the proportion of introverts was 25%, but the actual ratio based on the first official random sample by the Myers–Briggs organisation in 1998 showed Introverts 50.7% and Extraverts 49.3% in the USA. For further information, see Isabel Briggs Myers, *MBTI Manual: A Guide to the Development and Use of the Myers–Briggs Type Indicator* (Sunnyvale, CA, USA: Consulting Pyschologists Press, 1998).
If you would like to explore the MBTI tool within a Christian framework, CWR offers a training course (often called Understanding Yourself, Understanding Others). To find out more, visit www.cwr.org/courses
[2]A study conducted by Leslie Francis in 1991 found that the majority of 252 ordinands

and clergy were introverts. Further details of this study can be found in David Willows and John Swinton (Eds.), *Spiritual Dimensions of Pastoral Care: Practical Theology in a Multidisciplinary Context* (London: Jessica Kingsley Publishers, 2001), p68

[3]To read this article in full, visit www.lrhartley.com/seminars/stott-leadership.pdf

[4]Frank Tillapaugh, *The Church Unleashed* (Ventura, CA, USA: Regal Books, 1982)

[5]Visit www.frankviola.org and search for 'Rethinking Leadership in the New Testament'.

[6]John C. Maxwell, *Developing the Leader Within You* (Nashville, TN, USA: Thomas Nelson, 1993)

[7]John has recently published his memoirs about his experiences as a police commander. John Sutherland, *Blue: A Memoir – Keeping the Peace and Falling to Pieces* (London: Weidenfeld & Nicolson, 2017)

Chapter 6

[1]Garry Friesen and J. Robin Maxson, *Decision Making and the Will of God: A Biblical Alternative to the Traditional View* (Colorado Springs, CO, USA: Multnomah Books, 2004)

[2] Simon Sinek, *Start with Why: How Great Leaders Inspire Everyone To Take Action* (London: Penguin, 2011) (See chapter 5 in particular)

[3] Gary Keller, *The One Thing: The Surprisingly Simple Truth Behind Extraordinary Results* (London: John Murray Learning, 2014)

[4]Gary Keller, *ibid.*

Chapter 7

[1]*The Iron Lady*. Dir. Phyllida Lloyd. Pathé, 2011.

[2]Quoted in Henry Morris, *Men of Science, Men of God: Great Scientists who Believed in the Bible* (Green Forest, AR, USA: Master Books, 2012), p22.

[3]For more information, visit www.dwillard.org/articles

[4]John C. Maxwell, *Thinking for a Change* (Nashville, TN, USA: Center Street, 2005)

[5] Albert Ellis, 'Rational Psychotherapy', *The Journal of General Psychology*, 59 (1958), 35-49

[6]Teaching on learning to hear God's voice is beyond the scope of this book, but if this is something you wish to explore further, I recommend Dallas Willard, *Hearing God: Developing a Conversational Relationship with God* (San Francisco: HarperCollins, 2005) and Loren Cunningham, *Is That Really You, God?: Hearing the Voice of God* (Edmonds, WA, USA: YWAM Publishing, 2001)

[7]R. Rosenthal and L. Jacobson, 'Teachers' Expectancies: Determinants of Pupils' IQ Gains', *Psychological Reports* (19)(1963), 115–118

Chapter 8

[1]More of Mike's story is outlined in a book I edited and compiled. See Andy Peck, *God Unannounced* (Farnham: CWR, 2011)

Chapter 9

[1] Hugo and I explore the question of measuring discipleship progress in *Disciple Factory*, available on Kindle (2016).

Chapter 10

[1]Based on something I read in Chip and Dan Heath, *Switch: How to Change Things When Change is Hard* (London: Random House Business Books, 2011)

Information correct at time of writing (September 2017). All online content accessed September 2017.

Premier.

The author of this book, Andy Peck, presents a weekly show on Premier Christian Radio. *The Leadership File with Andy Peck* is broadcast on Sunday at 3:30pm.

Premier started as a London-based radio station in 1995. More than 20 years later it is a flourishing multi-media organisation including radio, magazines and interactive websites with on-demand video and audio.

As leaders in Christian communications, Premier exists to enable people to put their faith at the heart of daily life and bring Christ to their communities.

With an audience of more than one million people every week across the different media platforms, Premier represents a strong Christian voice in the UK. Its ministry includes campaigning on issues of concern to Christians. Campaigns have included e-safety (SafetyNet), slavery (Not For Sale) and ongoing issues with ISIS (Stop the Genocide), bringing a Christian voice to those in power.

Premier at a glance

ON RADIO:
- **Premier Christian Radio** nationally on DAB digital radio, Freeview and Medium Wave in London and Surrey.
- **Premier Praise** on national DAB digital radio.
- **Premier Gospel** on DAB digital radio in London and Surrey.
- There is a **Premier app** for smartphones and all stations can be listened to online.

IN PRINT:
- Premier *Christianity Magazine* helps readers connect with God, culture and other Christians through monthly articles, features and interviews.
- Premier *Youth and Childrens Work Magazine* delivers ideas, resources and guidance each month for those who work in children's and youth ministry.
- *Voice of Hope Magazine* is a quarterly update on the work of Premier and includes radio programme listings and daily scripture-based devotional readings.

ONLINE:
premier.org.uk is a gateway to content from all Premier brands, reflecting what is on air and in print and reacting quickly to current events. It includes video content of music, debates, interviews, resources, Bible readings and devotionals.

PREMIER ALSO OFFER:
- **Premier Lifeline** – a confidential telephone listening service for support and prayer every day between 9am and midnight on 0300 111 0101.
- **Premier Life** – an online lifestyle magazine inspiring people to make the most of life and its ups and downs.
- **Premier Jobsearch** – for those looking for salaried roles in the Christian, Charitable or Caring sectors.
- **Premier Digital** – inspiring, equipping and connecting Christians with digital technology.

More titles by Andy Peck

Coaching and Mentoring
Explore how to be a people-helper in two related but distinct ways: coaching and mentoring. Discover the similarities and differences between these two methods and how you can bring out the best in the people around you.

Small Group Essentials
Explore ten vital aspects of small group ministry, which will help you set a foundation for growth, discipleship and maturity in your groups.

Closing the Back Door of the Church
This book looks into why large numbers of believers have left their church or have never joined one, and discusses what could be done to combat the statistics reporting church decline.

Discover all titles by Andy Peck, current prices and more information at **www.cwr.org.uk/shop**

Courses and seminars for you

Our Pastoral Leadership and Small Group Central courses cover many topics specifically aimed at those in some form of leadership. We can also bring some of our courses to your church or small group and offer tailor-made teaching options.

Find out more about all our courses at **www.cwr.org.uk/courses**

SmallGroup central

All of our small group ideas and resources in one place

Online:

www.smallgroupcentral.org.uk
is filled with free video teaching, tools, articles and a whole host of ideas.

On the road:

A range of seminars themed for small groups can be brought to your local community. Contact us at **hello@smallgroupcentral.org.uk**

In print:

Books, study guides and DVDs covering an extensive list of themes, Bible books and life issues.

Find out more at:
www.smallgroupcentral.org.uk

Courses and events

Waverley Abbey College

Publishing and media

Conference facilities

Transforming lives

CWR's vision is to enable people to experience personal transformation through applying God's Word to their lives and relationships.

Our Bible-based training and resources help people around the world to:
• Grow in their walk with God
• Understand and apply Scripture to their lives
• Resource themselves and their church
• Develop pastoral care and counselling skills
• Train for leadership
• Strengthen relationships, marriage and family life and much more.

Our insightful writers provide daily Bible reading notes and other resources for all ages, and our experienced course designers and presenters have gained an international reputation for excellence and effectiveness.

CWR's Training and Conference Centre in Surrey, England, provides excellent facilities in idyllic settings – ideal for both learning and spiritual refreshment.

CWR Applying God's Word
to everyday life and relationships

CWR, Waverley Abbey House,
Waverley Lane, Farnham,
Surrey GU9 8EP, UK

Telephone: **+44 (0)1252 784700**
Email: **info@cwr.org.uk**
Website: **www.cwr.org.uk**

Registered Charity No. 294387
Company Registration No. 1990308